Praise for *30 Days to Social Media Success*

"Gail Martin Rocks! She gets to the heart of social media marketing. Packed with great information as well as a solid step-by-step strategy that will help you understand and apply social media. If you want to create massive value for others, get known, and take your business to the next level then this book is for you! Packed with information that works and makes sense."

—Wayne Lee, The Peak Performance Expert, *www.waynelee.com*

"Gail Martin has given all of us that are building our own business and overwhelmed about how to market using today's social media, a real gift. From page one, Gail lays out how to set goals, make a plan, and take consistent action. It feels like Gail is in the room with you walking you through this process step-by-step. This book is a must for anyone who wants to use the social media resources to build their business. And who doesn't want to do that? Thank you Gail."

—Cheri Britton, M.Ed _____ Room Thinking

"Gail Martin's 30 D _____ what you need to know to get free _____ Twitter, Facebook, and LinkedIn. She's spelle _____ short, easy format for busy people, so there's no excuse for not getting your social media marketing in gear. Best of all, this book explains how to use social media to build your business and how to contribute value to the online community. It's a must-read for any serious business owner."

—Jeff Crilley, president, Real News PR,
Emmy-winning former news reporter

"Anyone wishing to expertly grow their business by properly applying social media must read this book. Gail Martin holds nothing back and shares everything she knows to help you expertly move forward in today's world. This read is a must—for every business owner—who desires even greater success."

—Elinor Stutz, CEO Smooth Sale, LLC and author of *Hired!*

"Gail Martin is a brilliant marketer, especially in the area of social media. This book helps any novice or seasoned professional make sense out of all the social media confusion. If you want your marketing to skyrocket in your business, you will want to read this well-written and easy-to-read book."

—Ruth Klein, brand strategist and productivity coach

"This book is GOLD! Every small business owner or solo professional needs to read it. I can't believe how you explain how to get your social media marketing up and running in just 30 minutes a day. And these steps work!"

—Wayne Kelly, host/producer, *The Wayne and Jayne Show*

30 DAYS TO SOCIAL MEDIA SUCCESS

The 30 Day Results Guide to Making the
Most of Twitter, Blogging, LinkedIn,
and Facebook

By Gail Z. Martin

CAREER
PRESS

Pompton Plains, NJ

30 DAYS TO SOCIAL MEDIA SUCCESS
EDITED AND TYPESET BY DIANA GHAZZAWI
Cover design by Wes Youssi/M80 Design

To order this title, please call toll-free 1-800-CAREER-1 (NJ and Canada: 201-848-0310) to order using VISA or MasterCard, or for further infor-mation on books from Career Press.

The Career Press, Inc.
220 West Parkway, Unit 12
Pompton Plains, NJ 07444
www.careerpress.com

Library of Congress Cataloging-in-Publication Data
Martin, Gail, 1962-
    30 days to social media success : the 30 day results guide to making the most of Twitter, blogging, LinkedIn, and Facebook / by Gail Martin.
        p. cm.
    Includes index.
    ISBN 978-1-60163-130-5 -- ISBN 978-1-60163-719-2 (ebook)
        1. Internet marketing. 2. Public relations. 3. Online social networks. 4. Social media. I. Title. II. Title: Thirty days to social media success.
HF5415.1265.M329 2010
658.8'72--dc22
                                                                            2010025464

To my husband and children,
who believe in possibilities.

Contents

Author's Note

Preface

Today's small businesses and solo professionals live in an exciting time for marketers. Never before has it been possible for small and mid-sized companies without lavish budgets to utilize the same marketing tools as major corporations. Social media is equally accessible to "mom and pop" companies, one-person firms, and huge organizations.

Over the course of a year, I interact with thousands of business owners whose companies are at all levels of growth, from promising startups to established and mature firms, but all are looking for effective promotional tools that are also cost-efficient. Though social media is one of the most exciting new communication tools to emerge in the last twenty years and can provide effective and cost-efficient marketing, it's also one of the most misunderstood mediums.

As I travel around North America speaking to business and professional organizations, and as I lead teleseminars and online group coaching programs with participants from around the world, I notice that one question seems to dominate the conversation: "How can I use social media to really make a difference for my company?" These very busy people want hands-on advice with practical results, and they feel overwhelmed by the choices and the perception that it would take a huge time commitment to make social media pay off for them.

That's the reason for *30 Days to Social Media Success.*

This book is designed to help you create a strategic social media platform for your business, focused on reaching your best target audience in pursuit of your top business goal. Only you can determine your level of success, through consistent application of the tips and strategies I'll share with you in this book. Here's how I define success: being in the right places to meet with the people who are interested and able to purchase your products or services, engaging in a dialogue that meets your prospects' needs, and encouraging those prospects to become your customers.

The information and exercises you'll find in this book will put you well on the way toward achieving your social media goals. If you need more help or want to dig deeper, my Website at *www. GailMartinMarketing.com* offers a variety of options. I hope that you'll find me on Twitter, Facebook, and other social media sites, as well as on my Marketing Turnaround blog and Shared Dreams podcast to continue the conversation.

Now it's time for you to take the plunge into strategic social media. I hope it becomes a powerful tool to help you achieve your dreams.

Introduction

This book is dedicated to helping you rethink, reenergize, and restart your social media marketing in 30 days or less. If you're a coach, consultant, author, speaker, solo professional, or owner of a small or home-based business, and you can't afford to waste money or effort on social media marketing programs that don't produce results, this book is for you.

If you've never done social media marketing before, this is a great way to make sure you are starting off your marketing program on a sound footing. If you're using social media marketing but it hasn't delivered the outcomes that you want, this is a great way to retool your program. If your social media marketing is chugging along but not breaking records, this approach can rekindle and reenergize your efforts.

Let's get started!

First, the "guided tour." This book is designed with the busy professional in mind. The information is provided in bite-sized chapters that can be consumed like a daily vitamin for your business. Each day's "bite" covers one key step to reshaping your social media marketing in 30 days. Along with this important information, you'll also get:

~ Results Reminder tips on how to do it better.

~ The Rule of 30 approach to tap into a free source of marketing power.

~ Exercises to help you apply what you're learning immediately to your own situation.

~ A blank planning calendar on pages 200–201 to fill in as you go.

The RESULTS Approach

The RESULTS approach stands for:

Recommit to marketing.

Expect success.

Seek partners.

Understand your audience.

Look for win-win scenarios.

Take strategic action.

Stay visible.

The first step is to recommit to marketing. I've found that many companies that are disappointed in the results their marketing generates never actually made a full commitment to the activities needed to produce success. Half-hearted efforts produce disappointing results. In order to make this guide work for you, you must fully commit to putting the ideas into action.

The second step is to expect success. Your expectations shape reality, and they influence others on a subconscious level. Even if you put the ideas I'll share with you into action, if you do so without believing that they will actually work, that doubt will undermine everything you do. You will be preparing to fail. Having an expectation of success means that even if your first attempt doesn't produce the results you want, you will discover a better way to move forward from the lessons learned.

The third step is to seek partners. No one succeeds alone. Partners can take many forms. A partner can be a significant other who is invested in making your venture succeed, a virtual assistant, or a helpful ally. The most powerful partnerships are those you make formally and informally with other companies that are already serving your ideal target audience in non-competing ways.

The fourth step is to understand your audience. Many marketing efforts fail because they are focused on what the business wants to sell instead of what the target audience needs to solve an urgent problem. Once you align your marketing with the problems that are keeping your prospects up at night, you will be on your way to producing results.

Step five is to look for win-win scenarios. This means developing collaborative projects with your marketing partners to grow your business and theirs. For example, a certified public accountant (CPA) and a lawyer specializing in small-business law might team up to present a series of educational seminars on hot-topic issues involving money and law for small companies. If each firm already has an established opt-in e-mail list of clients and prospects, they could write articles for each other's newsletters. The firms aren't competitors because they don't provide the same services, but they do serve the same audience. Each firm wins through the cross-promotion, and the clients and prospects also win, assuming the information provided is valuable.

Step six is to take strategic chances. This book can't guarantee results. It can only share a system that has worked for me and for my clients during the last 25 years. Your effort is the only thing that can move results from a possibility to a reality. Results require risk. Your firm might grow larger, creating new management problems. Your book could become a best-seller—and then what? Demand for your product might exceed your current capacity to supply. More people are held back by a fear of success than by a fear of failure. (Reread that and try it on for size before moving on.) In order to really get results, you must be willing to take a chance. Your first attempt might not get off the ground, but the second try could be spectacular. Or you may succeed your way into a whole new set of problems. Either way, you have to take a risk to get results.

Finally, stay visible. Too many companies take the "prairie dog" approach to marketing, popping their heads up at random intervals and then disappearing again. Customers buy when the need is urgent for them, not when it's convenient for you. That's why you must stay visible through a consistent, ongoing program of marketing and publicity, not a few sporadic outbursts.

Marketing isn't mysterious. It's not difficult to understand the essentials, but it does take work to get results. You may have the good fortune to be able to delegate some of that work, or your checking account may dictate that, at least for now, you are a one-person show. Either way, as the company owner, practice principal, speaker, or author, you are and always will be your own most valuable marketing resource. This book will show you how to harness that power so that you can be efficient and effective and get the results you desire.

How the 30 Day Guide Works

Chapter 1 through Chapter 7 explain how to make sure your marketing is reflecting your true business goals. It's the underpinnings of the whole system to create results in 30 days.

Chapter 8 through Chapter 21 introduce the most popular social media sites and share my tips on how to use these sites to promote your business. By Day 21, you'll see how to apply what you've read toward specific business situations. You'll find ways to get your social media marketing off to a great start in just 30 days.

Chapter 22 through Chapter 30 tie your business goals and social media strategy together with other marketing actions for best results not just for 30 days, but all year long.

Why Most Marketing Fails

1

Marketing horror stories. You've probably heard them. You may have one yourself. These are the stories about how someone tried a marketing technique, sent out a press release, or ran an ad and "it didn't work."

I've heard plenty of these stories. And as with most urban legends, there's usually more to the story than meets the eye. If you're reading this book, you're a coach, consultant, speaker, author, or owner of a small business, and you want more from your marketing than you're currently getting. Or you may not be marketing at all because your business is new, or because you're afraid to fail. Or perhaps your marketing is chugging along with mediocre returns or muddled measurement.

Take heart. Marketing isn't mysterious, and once you understand how the pieces fit together, you'll be in a better position to market your own company or to oversee someone to handle marketing for you. Take the first step in the **RESULTS** model and recommit to marketing. Let's start by looking at the seven most common reasons that marketing plans fail:

~ No planning. This is true in both large and small businesses. Many marketing efforts fail because there is no link between the marketing actions and the bottom-line business plan goals that drive revenue. This happens because decision-makers get caught up with a vivid, creative idea that isn't accountable to the bottom line, or because they take a "great deal" offered by a salesperson for a media buy. Marketing without a plan is a disaster waiting to happen.

~ Inappropriate actions. If there is no plan, then whatever marketing actions that are taken may conflict with each other. It's unlikely they'll reinforce each other or support a business plan goal. Disappointing results come about because of a "ready, fire, aim" approach where actions aren't anchored to business objectives and target audiences. Attempts to copy a successful competitor's marketing without understanding why (or whether) the action is working for them is also a dangerous approach.

~ Lack of clarity about the target market. Mass marketing is dead. Blasting out marketing without a clear target is wasteful and unsuccessful. You can't hit a target if you haven't identified it. There is a sweet spot of potential customers who could become your ideal clients. You'll need to get to know them to win them.

~ Lack of clear goals. If you don't have an up-front understanding of what success will look like, you won't know when you achieve it. Not only do your marketing actions need to be linked to specific business goals, but each marketing action should be measurable. Build in measurability up front so expectations are clear.

~ Unreasonable expectations. A single press release isn't likely to create a big spike in sales. One ad probably won't save your company. Many people become disillusioned with marketing, because they don't understand the benchmarks for successful programs. For example, most direct-mail professionals are thrilled to get a 1-percent response rate. One percent! Yet many small businesses send out a postcard mailing and quit in disgust, expecting a response of 20 percent, 30 percent, or more. It's important to have realistic expectations so you recognize success when you see it.

~ Unclear on how marketing works. For many people, marketing is a lot like a DVD player: they don't know (and don't care) how it works. Your odds of creating successful marketing are slim without some knowledge of how the pieces function and the process required to pull the pieces together. With the Internet, new tools are emerging almost daily. You'll need to know how to blend New Media and Web 2.0 tools with traditional marketing to succeed in today's marketplace. Understanding what makes marketing tick is essential whether you're doing it yourself or delegating it to someone else.

~ Insufficient patience. "We ran an ad once and nothing happened." We've all heard that. But did you know that marketing research shows that it takes between seven to 30 "touches" to make a sale? Customers won't buy until they have an urgent need. Until then, all you can do is create name recognition and a good reputation. That's the value of the Rule of 30. Marketing has a lot in common with farming. You wouldn't plant seeds one day, then go out the next and dig them up in disgust because full-grown plants hadn't sprouted overnight. Seeds take time, and you can't hurry that. Marketing seeds also take time to grow.

Putting the 30 Day Guide to Use

Remember the **RESULTS** approach? In the next 30 days, you can see your social media marketing go from zero to full speed by applying the **RESULTS** formula.

Recommit to set aside at least 30 minutes each day (yes, weekends, too) to devote to developing your social media marketing strategy for the next 30 days. (Thirty minutes is a minimum. Once you get started, you'll want to spend an hour, so block out the time now.)

Expect success by throwing yourself whole-heartedly into this 30-day commitment. If the little voice in the back of your head keeps saying, "This is ridiculous. This isn't going to work," you are programming yourself for failure. Program yourself for success by writing down 30 things you would like to achieve from your social media strategy. Some ideas include:

~ Reconnect with old colleagues, friends, neighbors, and associates to broaden your active circle of contacts.

~ Attend the world's biggest 24/7 business networking event with a global audience (otherwise known as the Internet) and put your best foot forward.

~ Take advantage of all the free information, education, and competitive intelligence at your fingertips.

Now that you've seen those three examples, come up with your own list of 30 success expectations and keep them handy to check back on.

Seek partners. Social media is "social." You can meet amazing people on sites such as Facebook, and get access to experts you might not be able to reach any other way. Sites such as LinkedIn are particularly good for finding out what friends and colleagues are currently doing and who they know. Make a list of 30 friends, colleagues, and associates whom you've lost track of, and commit to finding them and touching base via social media.

Understand your audience in more profitable detail than ever before with the exercises in Chapter 3. Make a list of 30 things you wished you knew about your best customers, and create 30 questions you can use for quizzes, surveys, and social media discussions.

Look for win-win scenarios by posting valuable content on the right social media sites to attract more of your best prospects. You offer solutions, and they become your best clients. It's a win-win. Write down 30 ideas for useful tips, articles, videos, or other content you could post right away by reusing information you already have.

Take strategic action by putting what you learn in this book to work for you. As you read, be sure to do the exercises at the end of each chapter. Complete all 30 chapter exercises in the next 30 days and watch your social media soar!

Stay visible by keeping your social media sites fresh and relevant. Create a list of 30 upcoming events, newsworthy items, or announcements you could make to your new social media audience to get them talking, create dialogue, and demonstrate your credibility.

Most people put off doing marketing because they think it's too difficult or too time-consuming. By using the principles in this book, you'll do more in 30 minutes a day for 30 days than most business owners do all year. That's the Get Results secret weapon: strategic, consistent effort in pursuit of clear, measurable results.

Results Reminder

Planning + Effort + Consistency = Results

The Rule of 30

How many times are your messages touching prospects prior to making the sale? How close is that number to 30?

30

Exercises

1. Describe your primary target audience in detail: age, gender, education, location, income, key concerns, hobbies, aspirations, etc.

2. Justify why this is your primary audience. Now identify your secondary audience and explain why it's in second place. Look at your answers. Are they consistent with your ideal customer? With your current customers? How are they alike and different?

The Most Powerful Marketing Tool: The Business Plan

2

If the idea of creating a business plan makes your eyes glaze over, don't worry. This chapter isn't about the kind of detailed business plan you'd need to get a loan from a bank or money from a venture capitalist. In fact, the kind of business plan I'm going to show you just might be the most dynamic document you've ever created, and it is likely to be the most profitable.

First things first. If you've already written a business plan, print it out or dust it off and take a look at it. If it's more than two years old, its shelf life has expired. Why? The global economic changes in 2008 and 2009 require a whole new way of looking at the business world. Assumptions made based on market conditions prior to 2009 just aren't a clear picture of the real world anymore. So be prepared to make some changes.

If you've never written a business plan, you're about to find out how to make it your most powerful marketing tool. Pull out a pad of paper and a pen, and let's get started.

Define Success in Your Own Terms

Start off by defining what you mean by "success" for the next 12 months. There is no one definition for success. Success can mean different things to different people. Your definition should be what will satisfy you, and it's likely to evolve over time. But unless you know what your success target is for the immediate future, you won't know when you've hit it.

Here are some ways to define business success for any given year:

~ Profit.

~ Market share.

~ New product penetration.

~ Media coverage and endorsements.

~ National distribution channels.

~ Percent gain in product sales.

~ Industry credibility—speaking engagements, interviews, board or committee roles.

You may even think of a few more possibilities. The point is that success is more than just money, although for most companies and solo professionals, there is a target amount of money involved.

Ready, Aim...

Now write down your top three business goals for next year. Be sure to prioritize them from most important to least important. Do they match your definition of success?

One of the reasons marketing often fails for small businesses and solo professionals is that the marketing is not aligned with the prioritized business plan goals. Overwhelmed business owners take whatever marketing opportunities cross their paths, or buy into "deals" offered to them by persuasive media salespeople. They don't know how to say yes with confidence and no without guilt because they don't have any standard to judge the opportunities.

Your business plan sets that standard. Next to each of your prioritized business goals, I want you to write down who the target audience is for that goal. The more precisely you can narrow down the target audience (for example, instead of "everyone," it would be better to say "college-educated men between the ages of 18 and 30"), the more precisely you'll be able to target your marketing. You may have more than one target audience for each goal (for now), or you may have the same target audience for all of your goals. That's okay. We'll look at your audiences in more detail in the next chapter.

...Fire! Or Aim Again

Once you've matched an audience with a prioritized goal, make a list of all your current marketing efforts. List everything: Website, direct mail, print or radio ads, signage, social media, e-mail newsletters, speaking appearances, press releases, etc. Now that you've made a comprehensive list, match each marketing effort to the target audience it reaches, and to the business goal it supports. Do you see any disconnects?

Usually at this point, business owners notice that they have marketing efforts that reach a particular target audience but that they aren't communicating a message that supports the business goal that is now linked to that audience. For example, perhaps paid magazine ads are reaching the right type of reader, but the call to action isn't aligned with the top business goal, so if the goal is "increase the mailing list with opt-ins," the ad should encourage readers to go to the Website and sign up with their e-mail address to receive something.

Or business owners discover "orphan" marketing efforts that don't seem to connect with any prioritized business goal. Orphan marketing efforts might exist out of habit, or because they met an old need, or because there's an emotional connection to the action or to the person who sold it to you. But if it's not advancing a business goal, it's an orphan because there is no reason to keep doing it. They might also find marketing that is communicating the right message for a goal, but to the wrong audience.

Getting the message in sync with the best target audience in support of the right prioritized goal is the first step to marketing success. And though this book focuses on social media marketing, that's just one of many tools to help your company promote itself.

Social media marketing will be most successful if it's linked to the right goal and audience, and you'll get a multiplier effect on all of your marketing efforts if they are all in sync. As you'll see when we get into the details of social media marketing, good social media helps to send prospects to your Website, shares your press releases, or distributes your podcasts or blog posts. If those marketing actions aren't tied to the right goals and audiences, you can have a brilliant social media strategy but your prospect will get a muddled, ineffective message that will cost you sales.

Look for Gaps

Now that you've aligned your business plan goals according to your success priorities, matched the goals to the right target audiences, and matched your current marketing efforts to the right audience and goal, it's time to go "gap hunting."

Here's how to gap hunt:

~ Are there any goals/audiences without even one marketing effort?

~ Are all the marketing efforts bunched up around one goal?

~ Does most of your marketing effort support your top prioritized goal?

~ Is most of your effort being put into goals you've ranked as second or third in importance?

~ Do you have target audiences who aren't the focus of any marketing?

~ Is one target audience getting all the marketing messages?

~ Are second- or third-goal audiences getting more marketing messages than your top-goal audience?

Make a list of these marketing gaps, because you'll need to address them across your marketing, and you'll want to look for ways social media can help you plug the holes.

Defining Your Transformative Value

Before any customer spends money, he or she has to overcome two obstacles: ego and money. Ego is what makes people try to fix a problem themselves with what they have, rather than hire someone to do it. They don't agree to buy a service or product until they fail at fixing the problem themselves. Money is what clients hope to save by doing the job themselves. Most people won't hire someone for any job until 1) they have failed to do it themselves, and 2) there is enough at stake that continued failure will cost more than paying for the job.

Every person who buys your product or service does so because he or she has a problem. For example, if you are a business coach who specializes in work/life balance, your clients set aside time and money to work with you because they are currently out of balance. If you run a roofing firm, clients hire you to replace missing shingles. "Balance" or "missing shingles" is the problem.

Behind the problem is a pain. That's the chance that the problem could get bigger. The work/life balance problem could begin to impact a person's relationships or the ability to complete projects. A few missing shingles could lead to water damage and more expensive repairs if not fixed promptly.

Underneath the pain is a fear. The fear is the "what if" that keeps a prospect up at night envisioning the worst scenario. The work/life balance issue could lead to a divorce, delinquent children, or bankruptcy. Water damage could mean a whole new roof and expensive structural damage.

Your Transformative Value is the way you speak to the problem/pain/fear in your own unique way. When you make a sale, it's because you have done two things: successfully answered the ego/money challenge and satisfied the problem/pain/fear issue. To satisfy the ego/money challenge, you've convinced the prospect that you have skills they don't, you will save them money, and they'll have better results. You've resolved the problem/pain/fear issue by assuring them that you can fix the initial problem so well that the pain and fear disappear.

Successful marketing communicates your unique Transformative Value to your best prospects to satisfy both the ego/money objection and to solve the problem/pain/fear. Social media is one of the many marketing channels you can use to communicate that message effectively.

Results Reminder

Put most of your marketing effort into achieving your number-one business goal.

Rule of 30

Can you identify 30 ways your marketing speaks to your Transformative Value?

30

Exercises

1. Prioritize your top three business goals.

2. Match them to their target audience.

3. Match the marketing to the goals and audience, and gap hunt.

4. Determine the Transformative Value for each goal and audience.

Digging Into the Business Plan for Marketing Gold

Let's spend a little more time talking about your target audiences before we move on, because the key to all marketing is to give the right message to the right person. That's especially important in social media, because the "social" part means you are interacting with people, even though you can't see them face-to-face.

The first truth about marketing is that it's easier and more cost-efficient to go where your best target audience is already congregating, rather than trying to get them to form a new group. That's the thinking presented by magazine, television, and radio salespeople who show you a media kit that details who reads, watches, or listens to their product. The same thinking is true of events and social media sites. It's easier if you address a group that already exists rather than spending time and effort to build a brand new group and attract people to it.

Unfortunately, most small businesses and solo professionals have been so busy handling whatever business comes in the door that they haven't stopped to really think about who their best customers really are. Even fewer have thought about who their customers *should be* in order to achieve their business goals.

Getting to Know All About You

In Chapter 1, you wrote down a lot of details about your target audience. Take out that list, and compare it to the goal/audience/marketing notes you made in Chapter 2.

Here are some questions to ask:

~ Does your original audience profile match your new goal, audience, and marketing notes?

~ Are there second- or third-level audiences you need to describe?

~ How well do the target audiences you have described match your current core customers? What are the similarities? What are the differences?

Now think about those prioritized business goals again. Your number-one business goal should reflect your definition for success this year. Is your current core customer likely to help you achieve your business goal?

Let me give you an example: Suppose you're a life coach, someone who helps people clarify their vision of success for their business or career. Right now, your calendar is full of people you coach for one or two one-hour sessions and then move on. Very few of them return as clients after their initial sessions. They like you and appreciate the results, but they say money is the reason they stop after just a few sessions.

Now suppose you have as your top business goal to take your clients further through a new five-week coaching program. You would like to charge more for the program than you do for the regular coaching sessions, and your goal consists of two desirable outcomes: making more income from the same amount of time and locking in a longer income stream.

As happy as you've been with your current core customers, and as pleased as they've been with your work, it's not likely that they will be the best target audience for your new program. Why? It's probably out of their price range. That means you'll need to identify a new target audience for your business goal that is interested in what you have to offer and that can pay your increased price.

You also need to think about the clients you currently have who don't fit any of your business-goal target audiences. Maybe they were among your first clients when you started your business, and your vision has changed as time moved on. Perhaps you took whoever walked in the door. Maybe some of them haven't been pleasant or profitable, or maybe the work you're doing for them no longer fits with your goals. You'll want to take a good look at their characteristics to avoid attracting more problem clients, and you certainly don't want to make them a target audience. It's your call as to whether you gently let them know that you can no longer serve their needs or whether you just let them gradually drift away, but it's just as helpful to be clear about who you _don't_ want as it is to know specifically who you _do_ want.

For any of your marketing to work at peak effectiveness, it needs to focus not just on an audience that _could_ buy your product, but on the audience that is the _absolute best match_ for your product. There will always be some less-than-perfect clients who slip in around the edges, but you don't want to market to them. You want to market to your best customer.

People who were your best customer when you started out may not still be a good fit as your company grows and your goals change. That's okay. It's part of the life cycle of a business. You will save yourself time, energy, and money by knowing as much as you can about your best customer so that your message will be on-target to solve their problem/pain/fear. One of the scariest things for business owners is to shift their marketing from an original target audience that met their needs when they were a startup to a more precisely targeted audience that meets their evolving business goals. But unless you change your audience to suit your goals, your marketing is doomed to failure. Your outgrown audience just won't be able to meet your business needs, because your needs aren't in sync with their needs anymore.

Make the shift by thinking about the qualities your new best target audience would have—their goals, visions, and pains/problems/fears. What will get them past the ego/money wall? Now start to think about where those new audience members are already congregating. What kind of events are they going to? What clubs or associations do they belong to? What social media sites would attract them? Are they getting their information online or through traditional media? Now is a good time to update your goals and target audiences with what you've just learned.

SWOT Your Company

When you first started your company, if you're like a lot of small companies, solo professionals, and home-based businesses, you focused on what you did best that people would pay for, and you may not have thought much about the competition. Now's a good time.

Think about the other companies you've encountered who provide products or services similar to yours. They could be local, regional, or national. The scope is determined by where your prospects are looking to find solutions more than it is by whether or not you consider yourself to be a regional or national company.

Here are some things to consider:

~ How many other companies provide a similar service locally?

~ How far will my prospects drive to obtain what I sell?

~ Can my prospects get what they need online or over the phone? (If so, you're competing regionally and nationally.)

~ What's different about my product, service, and/or delivery than what my competitors offer?

~ What's very similar?

~ How are the companies I admire providing the types of products or services I'd like to provide a few years from now?

~ How are other companies offering value and convenience?

~ How do my materials or Website compare in professionalism to my competitors?

~ What's special about the things I offer or the way I do business to make my target prospect pick me over someone else?

Now that you've put your thinking cap on, it's time to SWOT your company. Take a piece of paper and divide it into four equal boxes. Mark the boxes "Strengths," "Weaknesses," "Opportunities," and "Threats." Now fill in the boxes from what you've just learned about your company and your competitors.

As you focus your marketing message, you'll want to emphasize your unique strengths (which include your Transformational Value) and go after opportunities (including your new best customers or overlooked pockets of customers who need what you have to sell). At the same time, you will need to be aware of your weaknesses and watch out for threats.

Remember when I told you that everyone has a different definition for success? It's true about weaknesses and threats, too. One "weakness" of your business may be that competitors sell at a lower price. But if your price is justified by superior craftsmanship or materials, you could turn that weakness into a strength, one that becomes a threat to your competitor's lower-quality product.

Threats, also, are a matter of perspective. If you are a personal trainer, you might think that every other personal trainer in town is a threat. However, the truth is that many of those trainers aren't going after your target customer because they're chasing a different target that fits their specific goals. For example, if you specialize in helping women stay active during and after pregnancy, and another trainer specializes in training busy female executives, you might turn that "threat" into a great two-way referral source as you refer clients back and forth to each other as the clients go on maternity leave and return to the workplace.

Results Reminder

Know your competitors and your best customers as well as you know yourself.

Rule of 30:

What are 30 characteristics of the prospects who best fit your number-one goal?

30

Exercises

1. Reassess your core customers in light of your prioritized business goals.

2. Update your target audiences to be the best prospects for achieving your new goals.

3. Now that you know your SWOT, look for hidden opportunities and strengths. For example, a high-integrity competitor might become a partner for collaboration, which turns a former threat into an ally. A current weakness might become a strength with a little adjustment. For example, a company that doesn't have a physical headquarters might think of that as a weakness, or they could reposition their ability to work with telecommuting staff and do virtual work for clients around the world as a strength.

Mining Gems From the Business Plan

4

Now that you're clear on your goals, priorities, target audience, and SWOT, it's time to talk about money.

Budgeting Time and Money

Successful marketing takes either cash or a "cash equivalent." A cash equivalent is what you use instead of cash. That could be time that you barter, but, more often than not, it's old-fashioned elbow grease. Marketing requires time, and it also requires some money. If you have more time, you can save money. If you have less time, you can get the same work done by hiring help. One way or another, good marketing is going to cost you.

I've heard business owners say that they had such a great location or product that they could "do business by accident." And I've driven past their location when it went up for sale after they went out of business. Success happens because of hard work, strategy, and, yes, a little optimized luck. It doesn't happen by accident.

What do I mean by "optimized luck"? Optimized luck is what happens when you've done your homework and worked as hard as you can, and a great opportunity opens up in front of you. If you hadn't prepared yourself, you wouldn't be ready to make the most of the opportunity, or you might not even notice it. But you also didn't just get lucky. You prepared and trained so that you'd recognize luck when it showed up and so you would be ready to maximize your big break. It's definitely not doing business by accident.

Take another look at your prioritized goals/target audiences/current marketing actions. If you've made a table, add another column for "cost." Write down what you think your current marketing actions to reach that target audience and achieve that goal are costing you. The cost could be in time, or it could be in real money. It could be the cost of hiring someone to update your Website or design your brochure, or it could include printing, postage, advertising, and other fees. You could include membership dues for the groups you've joined to mingle with your target audience. Make the best estimates you can and then look at the results.

Here are a few questions to ask yourself:

~   How much are you currently spending for each goal?
~   Are you spending the most to achieve your top goal?
~   Is what you're spending worth the potential new revenue that goal could provide?
~   Could you spend more if it would achieve your goal faster?

You may see some opportunities to make a few course corrections. If you are spending more to achieve your third priority than you are for your top priority, you've got a problem. If you're spending more to achieve a goal with smaller revenue potential than for a goal with larger revenue potential, it's time to reconsider. If you're not spending anything, hoping to do business by accident, then you're on thin ice.

Social media is "free" in terms of not costing money to sign up for sites like Facebook and Twitter, but it's certainly not "free" in terms of the time it takes to put a social media marketing strategy into action. You won't do business by accident just because you slap together a Facebook page or set up a Twitter account. If you don't have time, you'll need the cash to hire someone who can put the time into it for you. And if you have the time to put your social media marketing strategy into action, you'll still need some cash to bring all the pieces of your marketing plan together, so that your marketing works harder than ever to achieve your goals.

How Much Is Enough?

I've seen all kinds of estimates on how much a marketing budget should be. Usually, the estimate is just enough to cover the products or services the person doing the estimate wants to sell.

An industry standard that's been around for a long time is 5 percent of revenue. The idea behind making your marketing budget a percentage of your revenue is that marketing costs are funds you are reinvesting into the company, and should be tied to how well the company is doing. In the real world, I've seen companies spend far less and far more than 5 percent and get results that met their definition of success. What matters most is that you spend the budget you do have wisely.

A zero budget won't keep you in business long, and it certainly won't help you grow. If you truly have no cash, you'll need to roll up your sleeves and put sweat equity to work. If this describes your situation, how many hours can you put into doing marketing? Write it down, and put a dollar estimate of your hourly rate next to it. That's what you're really spending.

If you're already spending money and you're comfortable with that level of investment, make sure that you've prioritized your budget in line with your prioritized goals. Put the biggest chunk of money where you'll get the best return or achieve the biggest goal. (This becomes a great way to say no without guilt to one of those "fabulous" marketing opportunities a salesman presents to you.)

If you're willing to invest more to achieve your goals faster, or because you know that growth requires more resources, then determine a dollar amount you can spend and divide it among your prioritized goals. Budgeting money doesn't obligate you to spend it, but it does give you a tool to prioritize new opportunities, and it may free you to investigate options you might not have considered before you knew what was available to spend.

Remember that your marketing efforts must be accounted for in your budget either in dollars or in time spent. As you budget your time to complete other projects, be sure to allow for your marketing investment. Setting a budget also creates one way to measure effectiveness. Through time, you'll want to ask yourself whether a particular marketing method is earning its keep. Knowing what you've budgeted for it compared to the value of how it contributes to achieving your goal comes in handy when you need to decide what to keep and what to change.

The Irresistible Difference

Before we leave the nitty-gritty if your business plan, there's one item left we need to talk about: your "Irresistible Difference." You already know your Transformational Value. That's how you address your prospect's problem/pain/fear and overcome his ego/money objection. Your Irresistible Difference is what draws a prospect to you and your company as opposed to your competitors. Your Irresistible Difference should tap directly into who your best prospect or customer is. It should fit that customer like his or her favorite pair of jeans, not only covering what's necessary, but making them feel wonderful as well.

Go back to your best customer's qualities. What can you provide in your service, package, or delivery that will meet their need as well as their unspoken desire? For some customers, convenience is king. For others, it's value, reliability, or exceptional knowledge. Not only will you gain some good insights into powerful marketing copy by looking for the Irresistible Difference, but you'll also get some great ideas for where to find your best prospects and how to reach them.

For example, customers who prize value may join online communities dedicated to saving money. Those could be great places for you to participate through chat, forum posts, and blogs, because your audience is already there. A brand-conscious customer may place more than the usual value in being a member of professional and alumni associations and participating at a higher-than-average level. You might find those groups particularly useful to your marketing strategy, because they tap into qualities the prospect prizes.

Your Irresistible Difference demonstrates how well you understand the values your prospect has through where you market (including your choice of social media sites and the type of content you share), how you structure your product/service, how you deliver your product, and how you position your company in the marketplace.

As you become aware of the Irresistible Difference you offer to your different target audiences, make a note of it so you won't forget to put its power to work for you.

Results Reminder

Effective marketing isn't free. Prioritize your money, time, and effort, and make it count.

Rule of 30

What are 30 different ways you could illustrate your Irresistible Difference to your prospects and customers?

30

Exercises

1. Determine your marketing budget for each prioritized business goal. Make sure the biggest budget supports the top goal.

2. Figure out what you can really spend on marketing this year in time and money. Split that among your prioritized goals.

3. Identify your Irresistible Difference and start thinking about where your best prospects are already congregating.

Creating an Action Plan

5

Now you're ready to create an action plan for your marketing. Your action plan is the key to the rest of your 30-day success because it's your map and your to-do list.

Your action plan takes all the pieces you've put together so far and creates a way for you to make them happen. You won't achieve every item on your action plan in 30 days, but you can lay the groundwork to achieve them and make real progress toward your goal.

To be successful, your action plan needs to be detailed. Vague goals, such as "I want to bring in more business," are not helpful, because they lack the detail to enable you to take action toward making the goal a reality.

Action plan items must also advance at least one business plan goal by addressing that goal's target audience. You've already attached marketing actions to each goal/audience. This is a good time to look at those marketing actions and break them into smaller steps. That will give you a better idea of the time and money—and specific actions—necessary to make them happen.

For example, perhaps your top business plan goal is to get more visibility about your products and services. You've identified the target audience, and you've put "set up my social media site" next to the marketing action. That's a step in the right direction, but not enough to really get you going.

Let's break "set up my social media marketing site" into several action steps.

~ Identify one to three social media sites that already reach your target audience.

~ Sign up for your own page on each of those sites, with a user name that makes it easy for people to find you.

~ Gather the basic tools to set up your profile: current digital photo, short bio, and links to your Website and blog.

~ Read the rules and the terms of service so you don't accidentally get your account suspended.

~ Look for pages of other businesspeople, competitors, or top industry pros to see what they're doing with the site. Make a list of what you like and what you could do that's similar.

~ Check out the kind of comments and questions people are asking on other people's business pages. What kind of conversation would you like to start?

~ Visit the groups that relate to your area of expertise. How many are there? How many people are in each group? Who's leading the groups, and are they professionals or dedicated amateurs? How frequently are people visiting and posting in the groups.

~ Now get to know the options for building your page. Find out what kind of content you can post, what the file size limits are, and what extra gadgets you can add.

~ Get your basic page set up. Fill out your profile, and upload some content, such as articles, news items, tips, forum questions, photos, video, quizzes, or surveys.

~ Invite 30 people a day to be your friend or follower, starting with the people who are already in your e-mail address book, newsletter opt-in database, customer list, and card file.

~ Add something new or answer a question at least twice a week as part of your 30-minutes-a-day commitment.

Do you see how action steps take your marketing from being a great idea to something you can check off your to-do list and feel like you're seeing results? As you read through the rest of the chapters in the book, don't just write down marketing ideas. Turn those ideas into step-by-step action plans and attach them to the appropriate prioritized business goal and its target audience. This one step will make an amazing difference in the results you see from your social media marketing (and all your marketing), because it will make clear what you can do every day to make your goals happen.

Results Reminder

If a goal or a marketing strategy seems too daunting, break it down into action steps and then tackle one step at a time in sequential order to make it happen!

Rule of 30

Your daily 30 minutes for marketing should always advance or achieve one of your top-priority action plan items.

30

Exercise

Take a fresh look at the marketing actions you identified. Can you break each marketing action into at least three to five action plan steps that could be handled in 30 minutes a day?

Finding Your
Real Story and
True Voice

6

Have you ever noticed how some companies seem to change who they are and how they sound with every different marketing campaign? Even worse, have you ever seen a company portray a totally different personality depending on whether you go to their Website, read a brochure, see them at a trade show, or hear one of their commercials?

Many companies have a mish-mash of marketing materials that have been created over time, often by many different people. Some companies seem to lurch from strategy to strategy, never investing the time to allow any single approach to take root and pay off. Customers become confused, because the company doesn't seem to know its own identity. Even worse, a company that seems to change its personality every month can seem insincere, even untrustworthy.

The Internet complicates this disconnect, because it's easier than ever for prospects to hop from site to site, and if your company's personality seems to change between your Website, blog, online brochure, articles, and social media sites, your prospect will start to wonder who the "real" you is.

One of the easiest ways to fix this is to discover the Real Story of your company, and the True Voice that is uniquely yours. This technique works especially well in social media, because social media is designed to have a personal, conversational tone.

Telling Your Real Story

Remember the problem/pain/fear that drives your prospect past ego and money objections to seek out help? Your Real Story should demonstrate how you have solved a very similar problem/pain/fear for someone else, someone to whom the reader can relate.

The story format is especially powerful for sharing this information because human beings, even in the Internet age, are hard-wired to listen to stories. Stories sell. Social media is a perfect vehicle for telling stories, and it offers you a global audience. Not only that, but sites such as Facebook and Squidoo make it easy to tell your story with pictures, audio, and video as well as text. But first, you have to find the right story.

What is the story of your business? If you don't think your business has a story to tell, here are five ways to uncover your Real Story:

The owner's story. Some types of stories reach very deep into the American consciousness. Stories about second chances, self-made successes, hardworking newcomers who realize the American dream, and reinvention speak to very deeply held beliefs about who we are. I knew a business owner who came to the United States as an exchange student from China, and received her education and met her husband here. Because of the gift of a pearl necklace from an aunt back in China who knew a pearl farmer, this woman and her husband now own a pearl importing and jewelry design business. Her story of adaptation while retaining her roots has gotten her media coverage and positive exposure for her business.

The product's story. What need does your product meet? The owner of a chain of coin-operated laundries I knew realized that he doesn't just give people clean clothes—he helps them show their love for their families and succeed in the workplace by having a neat and clean appearance. In his city neighborhood of recent immigrants who are climbing the ladder of prosperity, family and self-respect are very deeply held values. Do your services or products offer people security, good health, or a chance to succeed? What is the need that prompts your customer to buy?

The story of your business. Has your business overcome adversity? We cheer for the businesses that found a way to come back after 9/11 in the TriBeCa neighborhood of New York City or after Hurricane Katrina in New Orleans. Has your company weathered bad times, lopsided competition, or succession crises, and come back stronger than ever? People love a comeback story (notice that Rocky Balboa has six movies!).

Your customers' stories. Go beyond testimonials. A case study tells the story of the problem and how your company solved it—but it's really a story about a hero, a dragon, and a damsel in distress. The dragon is the business problem—for example, a project badly behind schedule and over budget. Your company is the hero, and the client is the damsel in distress. Every good adventure has a few plot twists to keep our interest—what challenges happened on the way to slaying the dragon? Did you lose key project personnel when you needed them most? Did a piece of crucial equipment break or get delayed in shipping? Details like this make your story compelling. And then there's the happy ending: how your company solved the problem and what it meant for the customer (significant dollar savings, productivity enhancement, the ability to compete in new markets).

The story of your mission. Is your company part of your mission in life? Do you want to make the world a better place through the product or service you provide? Perhaps you became a lawyer because someone in your family was taken advantage of, and you want to make sure that others receive justice. Maybe you learned martial arts because you were robbed and ended up opening a studio to teach others to be safe. Your mission goes beyond your personal story to have a broader impact and make a difference in the world around you. Even the most mundane business can have a mission. Maybe you repair cars, but your commitment is to keep people from being endangered by breakdowns or from losing their jobs because of unreliable transportation. How do you make a difference?

Telling the Real Story of your business makes a powerful connection with potential customers. It can be the springboard to compelling media coverage. It can differentiate you from competitors in ways they can't copy. Once you uncover your Real Story, it affects the way you communicate about your business and the way you think about yourself, your products, and your customers.

The Power of Your True Voice

Many people put off marketing their companies because they don't feel authentic when they are in "sales mode," or they believe that marketing is inherently untruthful. How would you feel about doing marketing for your business if it felt completely authentic and truthful? Would you be able to overcome any childhood instructions not to blow your own horn if the words seemed natural, honest, and comfortable?

Using your True Voice to market your firm feels natural, sounds authentic, and just seems to flow. The True Voice of your business is in the words that seem to show up again and again in the way you describe your company, the way others introduce you and your company, and the way clients express their appreciation for what your company did for them. Many companies never recognize or harness their True Voice, so their marketing materials sound contrived, generic, or insincere.

Here are four tips to find and use the True Voice of your business:

~ Listen to yourself. The next time someone asks you to describe what you do or to tell them about your company, listen to yourself as you talk. If you have developed an "elevator speech," write it down and take a good look. What verbs are you using? What adjectives? What nouns? Make a list—you'll come back to it as you work through the tips.

~ Listen to your clients. Take some of your best clients to lunch and ask them to tell you what they like about your company. Explain that you are rethinking your marketing and want to make sure you are on target. Or, pull out the comment cards and e-mails sent by happy customers and look at the words they use. Once again, jot down the nouns, verbs, adjectives, and phrases that show up. Do some appear more than once? Underline the words and phrases that are used frequently.

~ Listen to your employees. Ask your best employees what they like most about what they do. Ask them to tell you about how they help customers. Ask them to describe the business and its products—and the solutions you provide. What problem or need do they think they are solving? Add the keywords and phrases to your list.

~ Listen to your friends. If you are introduced at a business function by one of your colleagues, what words does he or she use to describe your business and your service? What problem does he or she say you solve? Read over your own marketing materials. Do the same solutions or phrases pop up frequently? Write them down.

You now have a list of keywords and phrases that naturally describe what you do, who you serve, and what benefit you provide. To use your True Voice, take the most powerful words from your list and look for ways to use those words and phrases intentionally throughout your spoken and written communications.

When you use these True Voice words and phrases, you will feel honest and comfortable, because the words spring from who you really are and from the mission of your company. You'll find that the words make it easy to differentiate your services, because they come from your strengths and from the tangible benefits you have provided to your customers.

Intentionally using the True Voice of your business will make your social media message unique, compelling, and natural, and you'll feel more comfortable and confident sharing your information in a voice that feels right to you.

Results Reminder

Your Real Story told in your True Voice is memorable, credible, and compelling.

Rule of 30

What are 30 different words or phrases that come naturally as you talk about your product, service, and results?

30

Exercises

1. Identify your strongest Real Story. Now brainstorm ways you can share it through the power of social media. Text is good, but audio and video are also very powerful.

2. Be sure to look at your most successful brochures, Webpages and sales materials as you compile your list of 30 True Voice words and phrases.

3. Once you've compiled your list, keep it handy as you write blogs, Twitter tips, and content for your social media sites so you remember to use your True Voice words and phrases.

Touches to Transactions

7

Modern marketing wisdom holds that in today's advertising-saturated world, it takes at least seven to 30 touches or reminders before a consumer takes action. Although that may seem like a lot when you first hear it, if you think about how you act when you're the consumer, it begins to make sense. Your social media sites can account for several of those 30 touches. But to be effective, you need to think about how touches become transactions.

Touches and Trigger Points

We manage to ignore tens of thousands of advertising messages every day, mostly because they promote products we aren't currently interested in buying. The key phrase is "currently." When you realize you need a product or service, all of a sudden, you tune into the messages related to the product/ service that you had been screening out.

The situation that changes everything is a trigger point. It's an event that moves you from someone who hasn't thought about making a purchase or who has been casually window shopping to someone who needs to buy right now. The seller usually can't change the trigger point (although sellers try to influence it with sales and specials), but you can make sure you're making enough touches so that when a triggering event moves a prospect from looker to buyer, he or she thinks about your company.

Let's use a car purchase as an example. If your car is reasonably new and in good working order, you may not be thinking at all about buying a new car. You probably tune out car ads, e-mails from dealerships, or radio commercials about great specials. Or maybe you've been thinking about buying a new car—sometime. You might be casually reading car ads, going out to dealer Websites, paying some attention to commercials, even slowing down when you pass the dealer's lot for a good look. But for now, it's all still window shopping.

Then a triggering event occurs. Your existing car is in an accident, and it will cost more to fix it than it's worth. All of a sudden, you're in the market for a new car, and you need it right now. Until that triggering event happened, there wasn't much the car dealers could do to hurry up your purchase. You bought the car based on your schedule of when you needed one, not on the dealer's schedule of when he wanted to sell one. Business owners often forget that the purchase cycle is driven by the customers' need more than it is by sales and specials. But there's a very important thing to remember: when a customer moves from shopper to buyer, the company that has made the most marketing touches is first in line to get his or her business.

Go back to the car example. When that prospect was window shopping, the dealership with the best Website, or the showroom that was polite about a test drive without a commitment is likely to be the first place that prospect goes when he or she moves from shopper to buyer. Those "touches" pay off in top-of-mind awareness.

Where does social media come in? Social media offers a conversational, low-pressure way to remain in the forefront of a prospect's awareness with "touches" on a subject where there's interest but no trigger for an immediate purchase. It can also keep your company in touch with current customers so that when add-ons or upgrades become necessary, you're first in line for the business.

The key here is not to view social media as a way to provide a barrage of "buy now" messages. Instead, think of how you can engage the prospect in a conversation about whatever product or service you sell, with the immediate focus on offering helpful information related to the problem/pain/fear.

Some great examples of this are tips, how-to videos, short audios, links to interesting resources like articles, white papers, blog posts, longer videos, interviews, and question/answer sessions. Social media sites like Facebook make it easy for you to share multimedia content and have a two-way conversation about the topic in a format that reveals your company's personality and lets you share your Real Story in a no-pressure environment. Twitter is a great way to provide tips, ask questions, share links to related resources, comment on headlines related to your product or service, and even conduct surveys.

While you usually can't close a sale before the customer has experienced a trigger point, once you've established a relationship, you have the chance to educate the prospect about that trigger point. Perhaps the best time to buy a new piece of equipment isn't when the old equipment falls apart. Perhaps there are trade-in advantages or depreciation advantages to buying on a shorter purchase cycle. Maybe you can point out benefits that deal so much better with the problem/pain/fear than the old product does that the prospect decides to buy sooner rather than later. You've altered the trigger point through education, and because your company provided the information in an ongoing relationship, you're likely to be first in line to get the sale.

When someone subscribes to your blog, Facebook page, or Twitter feed, they're agreeing to get updates (information) from you on a regular basis. If you share information that speaks to his or her needs, every update does double duty: it reminds the prospect about you (a touch), and it provides useful information (deepening your relationship). Social media makes it easier and less expensive (and less intrusive) than ever before to stay in contact as touches prepare for a trigger.

Results Reminder

Using a touch strategy keeps you visible by providing useful information your targeted audience wants and needs without sales pressure.

Rule of 30

What content can you offer to provide 30 valuable touches?

30

Exercises

1. Your social media touches can introduce prospects to your Website, blog, or other sites. How could you use these touches to deepen your relationship with prospects?

2. Is there something you can offer prospects who have their triggering event that would provide value for their decision-making process?

3. What content can you communicate through social media that would increase your credibility and build trust prior to the prospect's triggering event?

Creating the Social Media Marketing Plan

8

It's time to take what you've learned and turn it into a plan for using social media as one of your key marketing tools. To do this, you'll use a combination of the things you've learned in Chapters 1 through 7 along with the new information you'll learn in the chapters that follow.

Pulling It All Together

Start with your business goals, target audience, marketing actions, and budget. If you haven't done so already, you might find it helpful to arrange this in a matrix like this:

Business Goal	Target Audience	Current Marketing	Budget	Social Media
Goal #1	Audience #1	Action 1, 2, 3	$$$	
Goal #2	Audience #2	Action 4, 5, 6	$$	

Notice that I've added a column for social media. As you learn about the major social media sites and their strengths, think about where those sites might fit into your marketing plan. Regardless of which sites you ultimately decide to become active with, they must fit the basic guidelines:

~ Advance a specific, prioritized business goal.
~ Speak to a specific target audience related to your prioritized business goals.
~ Reinforces or replaces marketing efforts tied to those goals/audiences.
~ Stays within the budget allotted for the goal/audience.

A word about social media and budget: Aren't most social media sites free? Yes, in terms of not having a membership fee. As you'll quickly find, social media takes elbow grease, and if you're not disciplined, all those interesting conversations can sap your time and distract you from getting other work done. There are also membership sites that work much like the free social media sites but serve specialized audiences, such as business owners and association members. These sites usually do charge some kind of monthly membership fee to access their forums, profiles, libraries, and directories of other members. If you find one of these paid sites and think it offers an ideal audience, be sure to factor in the yearly cost of membership as well as the time required to keep up an active presence on an additional site.

The next several chapters will go into detail on some of the most popular social media sites, including Facebook, LinkedIn, Squidoo, YouTube, and Twitter. Each of these sites has a distinct personality and culture. Because of that, they draw somewhat different audiences and have the ability to play unique roles in your marketing strategy. Keep your marketing plan matrix handy as you read, and jot notes to yourself on which social media site belongs with which business goal/audience, as well as ideas for how you might use the sites to reinforce or leverage your existing marketing efforts.

The Truth About Social Media

Despite the buzz that seems to be everywhere about social media, the truth is that social media is not single-handedly likely to turn your company around, make you a millionaire, or send your sales skyrocketing. Social media is a tool, in the same way public relations, events, radio ads, and direct mail are marketing tools.

Just like the power tools in your garage, some marketing tools are better suited for certain uses than others. In the hands of a master craftsman, a humble hammer and saw can craft an expensive piece of custom furniture. For most users, a hammer and saw can save money and increase value by handling home repair. The outcome depends on the skill of the user and the desired end result, although the tools are the same.

For a handful of "master artists," social media has been a path to fame and fortune. Many of those high-profile social media stars actually came to social media with well-established and very large opt-in e-mail lists, an established product line, a schedule of national speaking engagements, name recognition from prior business success, and the benefit of being among the first in an emerging medium. In other words, social media amplified the success they had already built elsewhere.

It's an important reality check, because there's still an "if you build it, they will come" fantasy that, all by itself, social media can make anyone a millionaire. The more you understand how social media works and the better able you are to craft sites and content that perfectly address your best target audience, the more successful you will be. Alas, there's no such thing as a free lunch, even on social media.

So what can social media do for your business and what can't it do? Here's a table for comparison:

What Social Media Can Do	What Social Media Can't Do
Raise your visibility to clients, prospects, and media.	Sell a product that is of poor quality or poorly positioned in the marketplace
Help you stay in touch more easily and with more frequency with valuable business contacts.	Make you an overnight millionaire.
Enable you to connect with people all around the world at a fraction of traditional costs.	Force people to buy a product that doesn't meet their needs.
Improve your search engine visibility.	Make up for a badly designed main Website.
Increase the likelihood of successfully connecting with reporters, bloggers, reviewers, and opinion leaders, who may endorse your product.	Guarantee your story will get picked up for front-page coverage on a big-name publication.
Introduce new prospects to your sales funnel and build your opt-in list.	Keep people listening if the message isn't relevant.

When used strategically with quality content and careful audience targeting, social media becomes a cost-effective, highly personal, adaptable, and relevant way to achieve all of the goals in the left-hand column of the table.

Social media works most effectively when it's backed up by a strong online and offline marketing program. For example, it won't help you much if your social media sites are brilliant at sending traffic to your Website if your Website isn't well-designed and can't convert windowshoppers to buyers or opt-in subscribers. You may do a great job of meeting prospects on social media, and perhaps even reporters and event producers, but remember that they will check out your whole package before deciding to do business with you. That's why it's so important to have a good Website, an opt-in newsletter, and some opt-in bonus downloads, online brochures, links to audios and videos, and a downloadable sales kit or speaking kit.

At the same time, a social media presence is becoming as expected for business as it is for companies to have a Website. Many consumers today would think twice about doing business with a company that didn't have some kind of Website. As more and more consumers begin to use social media as a regular part of their daily work and personal interaction, your absence will be noted as a negative.

Remember that when you join social media sites, you become the new kid on the block. You wouldn't move into a new neighborhood and begin pounding on your neighbors' doors to sell to them, so you shouldn't be aggressive in your new virtual neighborhood, either. Take the "community" part seriously and look for ways you can add value, help others, make connections, and have fun. Focus on being a valuable part of the community, and you'll be rewarded.

Social media is also a marketing essential, because it is one of the lowest-cost ways to network on a global scale around the clock. As you've seen, through downloads, audio, and video, social media can provide product sampling, while heightening your credibility and visibility.

A Few Myths About Social Media

Myth #1: Social media is just for kids. It's true that Facebook started out as a platform just for college students at select schools. But that's ancient history by Internet standards. Take a look on Facebook, YouTube, and Twitter, and you'll see marketing giants like the Mayo Clinic, AARP, 3M, and others who understand the value of being where their customers are already congregating.

Browse profiles, and you'll see that social media isn't just for teens. A large and growing percentage of users are older than 30 years old. There are no shortage of sites for midlife women, retirees, mid-career job changers, and others in their 40s, 50s, and older.

Myth #2: It's just a fad. That's what some music critics said about the four lads from Liverpool when they first appeared on *The*

Ed Sullivan Show, too. But like the Beatles, social media is here to stay, and it's becoming a powerful cultural force. Pundits acknowledge the role of social media in the 2008 U.S. presidential election, and major news organizations are actively soliciting reader-submitted news stories, videos, and live blogging from newsworthy events. Social media is now an established part of global communication, and you ignore it at your peril.

Myth #3: Social media is all you need. Rarely is it a good idea to use social media as your only marketing tool. Some of the first pioneering business users on social media have legendary success stories that will be very difficult for anyone to duplicate now that social media has become much more populated with competition. There is a distinct benefit to being the first in any new medium. The question isn't whether or not you can find a story about someone who used social media alone to build a marketing empire; it's whether you can achieve your prioritized business goals by adding social media to your marketing mix.

Myth #4: Quantity is more important than quality. You wouldn't get up in front of a national audience and ramble for hours without notes. You'd be squandering an opportunity. In the same way, slapping together as many social media sites as you can and then abandoning them is no substitute for a real social media strategy. Nor is cluttering up the site with unfocused content, personal musings, or political ranting. If you wouldn't say it in a business meeting or on TV, don't say it on social media. Use your marketing strategy to provide valuable content in support of your business goals to solve the problem/pain/fear in your target audience and limit the number of social media sites to those where you can actively participate on a regular basis.

Myth #5: I'm too busy to add social media. Like most things that are worth having, social media requires an investment of time and effort. Everyone is busy, but people make time for what they prioritize. That's the secret behind this 30 day guide. By allotting 30 minutes a day to social media for 30 days, you can get your social media strategy up and running. By continuing to invest 30 minutes a day (or by training an assistant to help you), you can expand that presence and reap the rewards.

Results Reminder

Social media is here to stay. How can you add value to achieve your goals?

The Rule of 30

Who are the first 30 contacts you will invite to your new site?

Exercise

The Sample 30 Day Social Media Marketing Plan

1. Read one chapter of this book every day. Then spend 30 minutes implementing what you've read.
2. Choose up to three of the social media sites described in this book. In 30 minutes a day over a few days you can:
   ~ Open an account.
   ~ Set up your profile.
   ~ Load initial copy, links, and other information.
   ~ Invite current clients, colleagues, and prospects from your e-mail address book.
   ~ Get to know the "neighborhood" by browsing other profiles, checking out interest groups, and seeing what other people post and what types of pages look professional and offer valuable content.
   ~ Read the rules so that you don't accidentally get your site removed or disabled by an administrator, and so that you avoid accidentally showing poor "netiquette."

3. Start compiling a list of themes and topics to discuss, tips to share, articles or videos to upload, or links to post. Add a few per week to keep your sites active.

4. Once you've invited as many of your "real life" contacts to be your friend or follow your site, gradually begin to invite other site users whom you don't know. Make the invitation personal and tied into a shared interest, such as an online or offline group membership.

5. Make it part of your 30-minute commitment to add up to 30 new people each time you're on. Don't go over that at one sitting, or you might trigger a reprimand designed to prevent spamming.

6. Begin to be part of the conversation. Allot 10 minutes of your time to find and comment on at least one blog or forum that has a topic related to your expertise. Be helpful and don't overtly promote. Always make sure you have a signature line that shares your company name, Website, and e-mail so someone who likes your post can find you.

7. Look for ways to add value. In addition to your own material, share links to relevant and interesting articles, blog posts, and videos related to your topic. Forward good comments, add insight into headlines that relate to your expertise, and be helpful.

8. Allow your personality to shine through with photos, videos, appropriate and professional humor, and your perspective on relevant current headlines. Keep it professional, but be a real person people would like to get to know better.

I'm on Facebook. Now What?

9

Facebook is like a global business-networking luncheon that is open 24/7. It's a site that encourages people to (politely) introduce themselves to strangers and invite them to become "friends." It makes it very easy to share multimedia information, making it much more valuable than the usual business card exchange. Not only that, but on Facebook there are interesting conversations going on around the clock and around the world where you can participate, add value, meet good prospects, and demonstrate your expertise.

Not That Kind of "Friend"

On Facebook, it's okay to talk to strangers. In fact, it's encouraged if you plan to use the site for business. If you went to a luncheon and only talked to people you already know, you wouldn't get much new business. It works the same on Facebook.

Some of the people who are your Facebook friends will be people you actually know in real life, either in person or via prior e-mail contact. Facebook is a valuable way to stay in touch with these contacts. But Facebook's real value comes in making it easy to meet people who might become customers and whom you might never meet in real life.

Of course, as with a live event, there are courtesies to be observed. That's one reason it's so important to read the rules up front, so that you understand the culture of a site and the expectations of its users. It's also a good idea to "lurk" for a while and watch what others do before jumping in. When you set out to meet new people on Facebook, look for something to indicate that they might be interested in your expertise or type of business.

There are two ways to do this: members of groups and friends of friends. When you join (or start) a group on a particular topic, odds are that the other members share an interest. So if you specialize in life coaching, joining groups on life balance, stress reduction, and navigating life transitions might be good to meet people with similar interests. You can also find a well-known author, speaker, or opinion leader who has a large following and introduce yourself to other "friends" of this expert as a fellow "friend" with shared interests.

What if someone you don't know "friends" you? It's okay. Treat it as you would at a networking meeting if someone new walked up and introduced himself. You would exchange polite conversation, share business card information, and explore how you might be able to help each other. You would not share personal or financial information or other "secure" information. Maintain the same kind of common sense in the online world, and you're unlikely to experience problems. If you do add a friend who becomes rude, intrusive, or inappropriate, you can block and "de-friend" that person easily.

Facebook and Business

If you intend to use your Facebook page primarily for business, set up a "fan" page which is a format designed for businesses. That way, if you also want a Facebook page just for personal use, you can create a personal page and keep it invitation-only for family and friends.

How can you use your Facebook page for business? Here are some ideas to get you started. (Add the ones that apply to your goals to your social media marketing matrix.)

~ Share tips, links to articles, short audios, and videos to enhance your credibility and solve problems.

~ Meet new people and keep in touch with existing clients, prospects, and colleagues.

~ Find and renew connections with coworkers and colleagues you've lost track of.

~ Invite your Facebook friends to online and real-life events, and post audio or video snippets of events afterward.

~ Post your Facebook address on your Website to invite visitors to join you online.

~ Use Facebook's photo feature to showcase case studies and other finished products.

~ Keep your Facebook site fresh by adding an RSS (Really Simple Syndication) feed that automatically posts your blog, Twitter, or podcast updates.

~ If you're already posting business video on YouTube or business photos on Flickr, you can easily add those posts to your Facebook page.

~ Get to know other users and make a reputation as a helpful expert by posting answers to forum questions and making meaningful contributions to group discussions. Better yet, start your own group!

~ Send virtual birthday cards for a personal touch.

~ Offer your products for sale in the Marketplace.

~ Liven things up with polls and quizzes you create.

Anatomy of a Facebook Page

~ **Home.** This is a page only you can see. It's your dashboard, where you can read your incoming messages, add applications, see what people have posted on your "wall," and change your settings.

~ **Profile.** This is the main page other people see. The information you add shows up here, as well as comments you approve for public visibility.

~ **"What's on your mind?"** This box works like Twitter, and it gives you the chance to send a short update. It's a great way to let readers know about upcoming events, news, and highlights. You can also use it to ask a question, tell readers about something interesting, or forward a link to a great article, blog post, or video.

~ **Wall.** This is the main public area of your site. You can make it so that you can allow your friends to post, or that only your posts show on the wall. To keep it focused on business, it's best to keep the wall showing your posts and comments on those posts.

~ **Info.** This tab shares your profile. You'll want to fill in the business-appropriate details, and avoid extras that are too personal. You can also share information about your education and business experience as well as links to your main Websites. Be sure to add a current business-appropriate photo. It's a key page to show your credibility!

~ **Notes.** You can have your blog posts feed to your wall, or add them on your notes page. Or, you can feed from Twitter to one and from a podcast or YouTube account to the other. It's a place you can post information with an RSS feed so your site gets updates automatically. You can also update your notes manually, like you would on a blog.

~ **Profile badge.** If you've seen the Facebook logo on someone else's Website along with their photo and a link to their Facebook page, this is how they created it. Great for linking your new page to your other sites.

~ **Boxes.** This tab is where all the other extras you add with the application tools will live on your page.

Customizing With Applications

Facebook offers a wide variety of extras that range from the very silly to the extremely useful. Because many people use Facebook exclusively to stay in touch with friends, there are extras that enable you to send your friend a virtual hug, a digital cocktail, and all kinds of personality surveys, among other wild and wacky things.

Though these are fun between friends, it's best to avoid them on your business site.

On the other hand, Facebook offers some great extras, called "applications," that let you customize your page and add value. Applications change all the time, and sites are always adding and deleting choices, but some are standards found in many of the top social media sites. Here are my favorite applications for business and ideas on how to use them:

~ **Events.** A great way to share your upcoming speaking engagements, teleseminars/webinars, seminars, and workshops.

~ **Videos.** Share your business videos, either by uploading them individually or using your YouTube page to update automatically.

~ **Photos.** Share pictures of finished products, photos from events, your book cover, and other visuals to bring your page to life.

~ **Groups.** The place to meet and connect with others who share a common interest.

~ **Broadcast.** A way to share your articles with all your Facebook friends.

~ **Blog RSS feeder.** Here's where you can enter the information necessary to have your blog, podcast, or Twitter feed automatically update your Facebook site.

~ **My LinkedIn profile.** If you're also on LinkedIn, you can create a shortcut to your public profile page.

~ **Squidoo Connect.** Make it easy for your Facebook friends to find your Squidoo lenses.

~ **Birthday cards.** Makes it easy to send a virtual card to all your Facebook friends on their birthdays.

~ **Memorable Web address.** Creates a Facebook "badge" you can place on your other sites to make it easy for visitors to find you on Facebook.

~ **Poll Daddy.** Add interest to your page by asking questions and posting the poll results.

~ **Marketplace.** If you offer tangible products for sale, this links you to an online retail page where you can pay to list your products.

Results Reminder

Use Facebook like a networking event that never ends.

Rule of 30

What 30 pieces of existing information could you add to your new Facebook page to make it more interesting and valuable?

30

Exercises

1. Implement items 2–8 on the Social Media Marketing Plan on pages 61–62 with your Facebook page.

2. Ask a half a dozen of your employees, real-life friends, and colleagues to comment on your page and suggest content, ideas for topics, and new ways to make it lively and fresh.

3. If you're in a creative field, investigate MySpace, another social media site that is popular with artists, musicians, authors, bands, and a more artistic crowd. Use the same strategies and tools to create your MySpace profile that you've learned in this chapter for Facebook.

Doing Business on LinkedIn

10

If Facebook is like a business networking luncheon, then LinkedIn is like a personal referral. LinkedIn is a great site for professional networking, and it can be a powerful tool to grow your business, but its culture is very different from the more social sites, and missteps on LinkedIn can be career-limiting.

On Facebook, Twitter, and many other social media sites, one of the main reasons to have an account is the opportunity to meet new people. On LinkedIn, the emphasis is on strengthening connections with people you already know fairly well. In fact, it's against the rules on LinkedIn to invite strangers without an introduction. That's because one of LinkedIn's greatest strengths is the power of personal referral and shared contact lists.

On LinkedIn, only the people whom you accept as connections can view your other contacts. Think of it as sharing the names in your BlackBerry or your business e-mail address book, and you can see why you want to limit access to people you trust. Because the culture assumes you know your connections well, it's okay to ask a friend to refer you to one of their other friends. As you can imagine, just as in real life, you'd want to know both parties in a personal referral well enough to not be embarrassed by inappropriate business behavior. That's why LinkedIn is an invitation-only, just for "real" friends site.

Though mass-friending isn't accepted on LinkedIn, there is provision for reaching out to someone you don't know. A basic profile on LinkedIn is free, but it's possible to pay for an upgrade that permits you to send a limited number of "InMails" to LinkedIn members without an introduction. (You can always InMail people who have accepted your invitation to connect.) Upgrades come in several levels, and prices and details vary. Because LinkedIn takes a very harsh view of anything spam-like, it's best to avoid contacting people you don't know until you're very familiar with the LinkedIn culture.

One of the most powerful features of LinkedIn is its ability to show your "six degrees of separation." Six degrees of separation is the idea that you are separated from anyone else in the world through only six personal referrals. LinkedIn alerts you to people with whom you share connections, suggesting that you either may already know this person and can connect directly, or that it's someone you may want to know through a referral by a mutual friend.

I'll give you an example of the power of LinkedIn. I was writing a chapter for a book and I needed to interview someone who had been instrumental in a product launch in California, someone I had never met. He no longer worked for the firm he had been with during the product launch, and that firm didn't know where he now worked. I looked him up on LinkedIn, and saw that we had a friend in common in New York City, someone I never would have guessed was connected. I InMailed my New York friend and asked for a referral. Within a few hours, I was set up to interview the contact in California.

Anatomy of a LinkedIn Page

~ **Home.** As with Facebook, this is your dashboard page. See your inbox, read status updates from your friends and groups, see who's recently been recommended, and take care of any edits or changes to your public pages. You can also give a one-line status update similar to a Tweet on Twitter.

~ **Profile.** Your public face. This is where you list your current and past employment and education (making it easier for old colleagues and classmates to find you). The summary you post introduces your connections to who you are and what you do. You can also include blog and Twitter feeds, links to your other sites, and all of your connections and recommendations.

~ **Contacts.** This tab shows all of your connections, and gives you the ability to import new connections from your e-mail list, organize your contacts into folders, and add or remove connections.

~ **Groups.** LinkedIn groups are especially powerful because people on LinkedIn actually know each other. Join LinkedIn chapters of your alumni organizations, professional associations, or industry groups. Posting useful questions and answers to your groups is a great way to meet other group members without risk. You can also start your own group. Be sure to join chapters of your membership associations outside your geographic location for extra benefit.

~ **Jobs.** This section lets you post a job for hire, manage the jobs you post, and apply for jobs others have posted.

~ **More.** Under this tab, you can search for contacts by company or industry, access the LinkedIn Answers page (a forum for asking and answering all kinds of business questions), go to the Learning Center to become a LinkedIn power-user, find out about live and virtual events, and access applications to customize your profile.

Customizing With Applications

Just as with Facebook, applications help you get more from your LinkedIn page. Because LinkedIn is all business, you won't find the virtual gardens or digital martinis like those on Facebook, but you will find useful apps to maximize your time:

- ~ Connect your blog, Twitter account, and events so that you can share them with your contacts.
- ~ Post your upcoming travel schedule and the events you are holding or attending, and find out what events your contacts will be attending and where they will be traveling.
- ~ Create virtual workspaces and share files, slideshows, and documents for online collaboration and virtual group meetings.
- ~ Find out what's being said about your company on the Internet.
- ~ Include your LinkedIn connections on polls and share the answers with your LinkedIn network.

Using LinkedIn (Carefully) for Marketing

LinkedIn can be a powerful marketing tool, but because its culture is very different from other social media sites, it's important to respect the rules and tread lightly. The best analogy would be successful in-person networking. You would never barge into someone's desk and raid their address book or BlackBerry. Ethical networkers also don't pretend to be referred by someone who hasn't given permission to use them as a referral. Apply that same networking etiquette on LinkedIn, and you'll be on your way to success.

What can you do to market your company on LinkedIn?

- ~ Create a profile that shows you and your experience at its best and most credible.
- ~ Use your Update box to let your contacts know about speaking engagements, new projects, or job-related news.
- ~ Use the My Travel app to share where you'll be traveling if it's important to you to make the best use of your travel time by fitting in lunches, coffee, and dinner with out-of-town contacts when you visit the area.
- ~ Use the Events application to invite your connections and increase your event visibility.

~ Be generous in giving (truthful) recommendations, and ask your contacts to write recommendations for you. Give first, and others will reciprocate.

~ Use caution in deciding who to add and whose invitations to accept so you protect the integrity of your connections.

~ Use the "six degrees of separation" indicator to ask your connections to refer you to others in their networks.

~ Use the Wordpress, Tweets, and BlogLink apps to have your blog, podcasts, videos, and Tweets automatically update your LinkedIn page to keep it fresh.

~ Fill out your profile completely, and use a good, recent, professional photo.

~ Offer to give referrals to your contacts, and introduce people you think might benefit from the connection.

~ Use polls to get snapshots of what your customers and prospects think about key issues. Polls can also help you gather statistics for reports and presentations.

~ Join groups and add value by participating in them. Virtual chapters of professional, industry, and alumni associations in which you're already a member are especially valuable.

~ Reconnect with mentors, colleagues, and subordinates whom you'd lost track of from prior companies. (The company and industry search functions are very helpful for this.) You expand your active network with people you already know.

~ Start a group if your key membership organizations aren't represented. If you remain active as a group leader, it can be a great way to remain visible.

~ Let your contacts know what kinds of new projects you're interested in, so they know if you're open to be approached.

Results Reminder

LinkedIn maximizes your personal business connections and leverages your six degrees of separation.

Rule of 30

For 30 days, invite your past and current colleagues, prospects, clients, subordinates, bosses, and contacts, and watch your sphere of influence grow!

30

Exercises

1. Write a great profile page. Fill out your former employment and alma maters so past colleagues can find you. Make your summary compelling. Use a good, current photo.

2. Watch LinkedIn's suggestion of people you may know based on shared connections to find colleagues you've forgotten to add.

3. Get involved with alumni, professional, or industry groups and make a reputation of being helpful and knowledgeable.

4. Add your best contacts, and invite your most promising new contacts as you meet people.

5. Be proactive in recommending people, and ask others to recommend you.

6. Ask for referrals sparingly, but don't be afraid to request help connecting if it's worth it.

The Twitter Revolution

11

If Facebook is a networking event and LinkedIn is like a personal referral from your BlackBerry address book, then Twitter is the cocktail party of the social media scene.

Twitter is a "microblogging" site, which means that it's like blogging, only shorter. On Twitter, users can share 140-character messages called Tweets. Thanks to an ever-growing number of applications and add-ons, you might be surprised at the power in those short Tweets to connect you to potential prospects and customers.

Where Facebook has friends and LinkedIn has connections, Twitter has followers. The easiest way to increase your number of followers is to either invite people you know from the real world (or other social media sites) to follow you, or to follow other people who share your interests and hope they follow you in return.

Who Are the People in
Your Neighborhood?

On Twitter, they're the people that you Tweet each day. Twitter is addictive, and lots of users check throughout the day for new and interesting posts. If you develop a reputation for providing useful, interesting content, they'll be checking for your posts and watching for your next Tweet.

Twitter is perfect for busy people, because the posts are short and sweet. Twitter also has a variety of ways you can interact with your followers and share valuable content. Just like workplace conversation around the water cooler, it's the content, not the duration, of the conversation that counts.

When it comes to finding other people to connect with on Twitter, start with people who are already part of your online and offline life. Twitter, like Facebook, takes the idea of friendship casually (unlike LinkedIn), so invite everyone. Your e-mail and BlackBerry address books are a great place to start, plus your opt-in newsletter list, and everyone you meet at live networking or business events. (Finding and friending or following people on Facebook and Twitter after meeting at a business function is a great way to stay in touch.)

So far, there isn't an automatic way to invite your Facebook friends to be Twitter followers other than posting in your "What's on your mind?" status box and making a general announcement and invitation. You can, however, add your Tweets via RSS through a Facebook application that automatically updates as you Tweet.

If you have a fan page on Facebook, you can use one of Facebook's applications to send your Facebook page updates to your Twitter account. (At press time, the application was only available for fan pages, not for personal accounts.)

Avoid the friend/follower frenzy. When it comes to Twitter (and Facebook), more isn't always better. Sure, you'll find celebrities and organizations with tens or hundreds of thousands of followers, even a million. That might be great for a movie star or a corporation, but for small-business marketing, bigger isn't always better. You want qualified followers, not just huge numbers. The whole reason you're on social media is to attract potential customers. It's better to have a few thousand friends/followers who are truly interested in you, your product, or your topic than to have tens of thousands of faux-followers who will never buy from you. That's a great reason to avoid the automated services that promise to add thousands of friends. Those programs don't provide a way to strategically choose who to friend or follow, so you're unlikely to get qualified prospects. Even worse, using automated following programs could get your account suspended. There's no substitute for choosing your own friends.

Anatomy of a Twitter Page

Twitter is stripped-down elegance. Where sites like Facebook offer you the opportunity to build out multiple tabs with photos and videos and content, Twitter is lean, but surprisingly powerful.

~ **Home.** This is your dashboard. From your Home page, you can add Tweets under "What's Happening?", see how many people you're following and how many are following you, and see how many people have added your Twitter site to a list of sites they follow. Home is also where you can send @Replies and Direct Messages, reTweet interesting content, list your favorites, or search for topics or people. Your Home page also gives you the top keywords people are Tweeting about so you can follow the trends and hot topics. You'll also find the RSS feed for your Twitter profile on your homepage (use this to add your Tweets to your other sites). And there are mini-photos of all your followers, so you can zoom in to find out what's new with specific people. On your Home page, you see Tweets from all your friends.

~ **Profile.** This is what other people see. On your profile page, you'll see just your own Tweets. This is the view you want to have show up on your other sites.

~ **Find People.** This page helps you add followers in several different ways. You can invite people, companies, or organizations by name, or you can invite your e-mail list. Find People also has a limited list of topics where you might find like-minded people. It's a good place to start when you begin to invite people you don't actually know. Important: Make sure you have read Twitter's rules (Terms) before you begin to add friends. Twitter takes a dim view of "mass friending" and can suspend your account for adding too many friends in a short period of time.

~ **Settings.** This is where you set up your one-line bio, indicate the contact information you're willing to share, and post your photo. You can also design the wallpaper around your Twitter page, indicate whether you want e-mails when people follow you, and lets you enable your mobile phone so you can Tweet from anywhere. The Connections tab gives you an update on which applications have access to your Twitter account.

~ **Blog.** At the bottom of the site is the link to the Twitter blog. It's a great place to find out what's going on with the Twitter site so you'll be the first to know about new features.

~ **Goodies.** Also at the bottom of the site is the Goodies page, which gives you access to Applications, Widgets, and Buttons. These extend Twitter's usefulness, help you connect Twitter to other sites, and give you more flexibility in how you use your Twitter account.

Navigating in Twitter

Twitter has its own language, and a few simple, but powerful, ways you can send messages. Here are the basics:

~ **@Username.** Makes a public reply to something that someone else Tweeted. A great way to keep a conversation going back and forth and to invite others to jump in.

~ **Direct Message (DM).** Sends a private message to someone who is following you.

~ **Hashtag (#).** Using a # in front of a keyword enables your Tweet to be searchable on Twitter, and if enough people are using that #keyword, it could make the Trending Topics list.

~ **ReTweet (RT).** A great way to share interesting Tweets someone else posted, and to give a promotional bump to your friends. Copying a message you received and leading with "RT @Username" will share that message, link, or information with your whole list.

Customizing Twitter With Applications

You'll find plenty of "100 Best Twitter App" sites and articles, demonstrating that there are as many different ways to use Twitter as there are people on Twitter. Most Twitter apps just give you the ability to track information, use Twitter for specific purposes, or share certain kinds of information. Some of the apps help you manage your Twitter page so that you can make better use of your time. Here are some of my favorites:

~ **SocialOomph.com (formerly TweetLater).** This site lets you load Tweets in advance and then schedule them over days or weeks. It's a lifesaver to help you keep a regular presence on Twitter when you have other things to do.

~ **TinyURL.com.** Because you only have 140 characters, sharing a link to a site, article, or video can be a problem. TinyURL generates a unique, small link perfect for Tweeting.

~ **Twibes.com.** Like groups on Facebook, Twibes is the place to join up with like-minded people or find people you'd like to meet.

~ **Strawpollnow.com.** Fun way to make your Twitter site interactive with yes/no polls and quizzes.

~ **Twellow.com.** A directory of people and organizations on Twitter, making it easier to find places to connect.

~ **TweetDeck.com.** Helps you manage all your Twitter connections.

~ **TweetBeep.com.** Like a Google Alert for Twitter, it helps you know when you and your products are being discussed.

~ **Twhirl.com.** Makes it easier to stay logged into Twitter all day to post updates and read new Tweets without having a browser open.

~ **Twitturly.com.** Helps you track what topics and keywords are getting the most discussion.

~ **Twitscoop.com.** Another way to find what everyone's talking about and join in to the high-buzz topics.

~ **TwitterFeed.com.** Makes it easy to have your blog and other sites update your Twitter page.

~ **NearbyTweets.com.** Find Twitter events and users close to your geographic area.

Once you start to use Twitter, you'll find more apps and add-ons that fit your specific needs, so enjoy exploring!

Using Twitter for Business

The key to using Twitter for business is to think about what you can share in 140 characters that your prospects/customers need. Here are some ideas to get you going:

~ Share short, actionable, and to-the-point tips related to your area of expertise—saving money, exercise, diet, marketing, reducing stress, living green.

~ Invite followers to live or virtual events.

~ Update followers on new blog posts or articles.

~ Invite discussion by posting a poll, asking a question, or having a trivia contest.

~ Stage a "Tweetup" or live event invitation via Twitter. They are great for more spontaneous get-togethers or telling your followers about in-person sales or discounts.

~ Publicize your "flavor of the day," whether it's a daily special, ice cream of the day, or a helpful tip.

~ Invite participation in real-time when you're on a live radio call-in show.

~ Notify followers if there's a last-minute event cancellation or weather-related store closing. If your Website goes down but you can get to a WiFi location, send out a Tweet to let followers know you'll be back up soon.

~ Offer a teaser by Tweeting the first paragraph of an article (with a link to the rest) or the first chapter of your new book.

~ Reward followers with links to special content, coupons, or first-look content.

~ Send Tweets from the road as you attend conferences and events. Make sure you use hashtags so your Tweets trend with others from the same event.

~ Watch Trending Topics to see where the buzz is, and jump into the conversation if you can add relevant information or insight.

~ Keep it interesting and helpful by reTweeting good posts by colleagues and opinion leaders; sending links to articles, blogs, and videos; and being on the lookout for great relevant content to share.

~ Follow your competitors or industry leaders to see what others are doing and borrow best practices.

Results Reminder

Turn articles and blog posts into a series of Tweets to re-use valuable content.

Rule of 30

Tweet regularly so your followers have a reason to stay tuned and reTweet! Can you come up with 30 useful and interesting Tweets to get started?

30

Exercises

1. Set up your Twitter account and invite 30 friends a day to be your followers.
2. Look for new contacts through shared interests and Twibes.
3. Don't forget to invite your Facebook friends and let your LinkedIn connections know you're on Twitter.
4. Better yet, link Facebook and LinkedIn to Twitter via RSS so your Tweets update your other pages automatically.
5. Create interesting Tweets from your articles and observations. Avoid a hard-sell approach. Offer tips; don't just sell.
6. Ask and reply to questions to build relationships.
7. Make it fun and interactive, while keeping it professional. Let your personality shine through.

Blogging for Business

12

In the short span of just a few years, blogging has become real competition for traditional news media, especially newspapers and magazines. What bloggers lack in professional reporters' credentials, they often make up for in access and passion. If you've missed out on blogging so far, this is a good time to get started. And if you've created a blog that hasn't caught on, now's the time to fix it!

Blogging Basics

A blog is a special kind of Webpage that is easy to update. There are a variety of free blogging platforms to choose from: Wordpress, Live Journal, and Blogger are just a few of the most popular. Before you sign up to start a blog, make sure you read the site's terms of service. Some sites frown on "commercial" blogs and will delete them. Make sure your blog is welcome before you invest time in creating a following.

Today's blogs make it easy to share more than just text. Videos, web links, photos, polls, and audio are easy to share or embed in your blog post. Blogging also makes it possible for you to get comments from readers and to create a two-way dialogue. You can share valuable information, post questions, and get the conversation going. And if you've ever thought about writing a book but thought it was too intimidating, try approaching your topic one blog post at a time and then pulling together your blog copy as the beginnings of a manuscript.

Anatomy of a Blog

~ **Dashboard.** This is your behind-the-scenes control panel. Dashboards will differ by site, but Wordpress's dashboard lets you know everything from how many posts you've made to how many people have visited your site. In addition to statistics, your dashboard is where you can change your settings, read comments, add new pages, change your blog's appearance, and add a new post. You can also get an idea of how many people are visiting your blog and which blog posts they're passing along to friends.

~ **Tags.** Tags are like keywords: they help search engines find your blog posts. Use tags that describe the key topics in your blog posts so that readers searching for similar information find your blog. Better yet, keyword tags related to top headlines are likely to show up when searchers look for what's in the news.

~ **Blogroll.** This is a list of other blogs you follow. It's a great way to do a favor for friends whose blogs you enjoy, because your readers may discover their blogs through your blogroll. You can also add blogs by newsmakers, opinion leaders, trendsetters, and industry mavens to help your readers connect to the larger blogsphere.

~ **Profile.** This is the way the site looks to everyone else. You'll see the posts, plus links to your other blog pages including your bio.

~ **Archives.** Share your previous posts with readers who missed out!

~ **Categories.** As you add blog posts, you can indicate the category each posts belongs in. This helps readers find relevant information.

~ **RSS.** Really Simple Syndication is the special code that enables you to feed your blog posts to your other sites such as Facebook and LinkedIn, or use your blog to add fresh content to your Website.

Why Blog?

With everything else a busy business owner has to do, what's the benefit in blogging? Here are some reasons for you to consider:

~ Because a blog is easy for you to update, you can add new content frequently without paying high fees to your Webmaster for changes.

~ Blogging creates a way for your to comment on life, business, trends, and issues that impact your field.

~ Blogging is a way to let your personality shine through and create a more personal connection.

~ Your blog can extend the information you share through articles, books, and speeches, and invite comments and dialogue.

~ Many bloggers have received national recognition based on the value of their content.

~ Good blog posts increase the Google search results for your name and company.

~ Guest blogging on the sites of friends and colleagues introduces you to their followers and is great visibility.

~ When you use your blog's RSS feature, you can easily update multiple Websites and social media sites with a single blog post.

Although there are no hard rules, it's generally held that "active" blogs are updated at least twice a week. Short posts are okay, and you can reuse content you've created for other purposes by chopping it into smaller bites. This gives new life and a new audience to articles, case studies, audios, videos, and white papers.

If you're blogging about topics related to current headlines, blog early (around 8 a.m. Eastern) to attract readers who get their online news and commentary with their morning coffee. However, your readers may have different Web-surfing patterns depending on how they use the Web. You may find that your readers log on over lunch, after supper, or even later (when the kids are in bed). To find out when the ideal time is to post, see what others who speak to your target audience are doing, or ask your customers, prospects, and Twitter followers when they spend time online.

Using Your Blog for Business

How can you use your blog to increase your Internet visibility, improve your search engine results, and drive more traffic to your Website (which stands a good chance of increasing your sales)? Here are some ideas:

- ~ Comment on headline news from your professional perspective. If you're a relationship coach, celebrity split-ups are good case studies. A financial consultant might provide real-life ways to reduce debt and save money. Talk about what everyone's already talking about.
- ~ Extend information you've already provided. If you've written a book, provide extra related material. If you write a column, go into additional details on a subject you've recently covered.
- ~ Share short case studies or brief tips.
- ~ Keep it fresh, current, and fun. Avoid long lags between posts and try to post at consistent times so readers know what to expect. Stay positive and realize that going on a rant lasts forever on the Internet, long after you've cooled down.
- ~ Choose snappy titles to increase readership, and write in short paragraphs.
- ~ Use social bookmarking sites like Digg, Delicious, and StumbleUpon to share your blog posts, and Tweet when you post so your Twitter followers will know.

~ Make it easy for your readers to share posts they like by adding bookmarking icons from AddThis.com.

~ Use RSS to feed your blog to your Website so your main site always has fresh content (which improves search engine rankings).

~ Consider getting together with a group of three to five other professionals in non-competing businesses that share the same target audience, and share a blog so no one has to do all the writing.

~ Keep an eye out for well-established blogs on your topic and suggest that you and the other blogger swap guest blogs. It's a great way to introduce both of you to the other's readership.

~ Be generous in linking good blogs to your blogroll, and don't be shy about asking other bloggers to add your blog to their blogroll.

~ Use tags and keywords to make your posts more searchable. Your keywords should relate to the post's copy, and to your overall topic. Not sure which words have the best traffic? Go to Google's Keyword Tool program (it's free). Google Keyword Tool gives you a list of the words associated with your topic and shows you how many times each word gets searched on Google. If you have a choice between two words that mean the same thing, and one gets a million searches and one gets a few thousand, start using the higher traffic word and get more hits on your blog posts!

~ Make your blogs helpful but don't come across like you're selling. Your blog is a way for readers to get to know you. If they like you and think you're credible, they'll consider buying from you.

~ Announce your upcoming events, speaking engagements, awards, and other news on your blog, but do it in a conversational way; don't just post press releases.

~ Use your blog to encourage readers to download free information off your Website, such as articles or e-books, to help build your opt-in list.

~ Realize that it takes months or years to build a follow-ing. Your goal as a business blogger isn't to have more readers than CNN. Your goal is to attract qualified pros-pects who can get to know you prior to doing business with you. You don't need huge numbers; you just want the right readers.

~ Blogs don't have to be for the general public. You can create a blog that is mainly for clients and users of the products you sell. Specialized blogs don't get huge num-bers of readers, but sources of good niche information can win loyal fans and future customers.

~ Blogging can have benefits other than boosting sales. You might attract a reporter's attention and be asked for an interview. A reader comment could spark an idea for a new column or an article you publish elsewhere. Blog posts could be assembled and edited into a book. Invitations to speak for groups or opportunities for col-laboration could arise out of great posts that catch the right person's attention. Remember that success isn't al-ways measured in product sales.

How to Get It All Done

There's more than one way to do the work it takes to keep a so-cial media strategy on track. Here are ways other professionals who blog manage their time:

~ Write once, and post everywhere. Assemble a group of articles, e-books, white papers, and speeches that you've written, and hire a staffer to edit them into blog posts. You can do the same thing by editing webinars and teleseminars into short (five minutes or less) segments and posting them as well.

~ Write a number of posts (and Tweets) in advance. It takes less time to post than to write, so if your sched-ule is full of peaks and valleys, use your down time to write posts and Tweets that you can upload later.

~ Use a virtual assistant to upload material you've written. You do the writing, and your virtual assistant handles the posting, tagging, keywords, and maintenance.

~ Assemble a group of like-minded professionals to group blog. Or invite guest bloggers on a regular basis.

~ Pick a day and time on a regular basis when you know it will be quiet and focus just on your blog for 30 minutes.

~ Call attention to great articles, blog postings, Tweets, videos, and essays by other people by posting a link to their information and adding a short commentary.

Results Reminder

Just like a garden, blogs and social media take time to earn a following. Focus on quality, not quantity.

The Rule of 30

An investment of 30 minutes twice a week should keep your blog fresh and keep you in touch with readers and comments.

30

Exercises

1. Make a list of all the written information (articles, books, e-books, case studies, white papers, etc.) you could re-purpose into blog posts.

2. Now make a list of the topics you would like to write about. Make sure it supports your number-one business goal and speaks to your top target audience.

3. Prioritize your topics by choosing those with ties to current headlines first to get the most impact.

4. For just 30 days, block out 30 minutes on two days each week to get your blog established. Even if you intend to have someone help you later, it's good to get the feel of it yourself.

5. Let everyone know about your blog by posting a link (or using RSS to feed your Website), including a link in your newsletter and e-mail signature, and sending out a press release.

Do You Squidoo?

13

Squidoo, the cool site with the funny name, is the brain-child of marketing guru Seth Godin. Squidoo works a little differently from most social media sites in that it allows you to create as many pages as you want (on Squidoo, pages are called "lenses") but it's not a site that focuses on massive friending and following. The emphasis is on the content, and having a Squidoo lens can be a great way to increase your traffic and search result if you understand the community.

Squidoo calls its pages lenses, because a lens focuses tightly on a particular subject, which is what it wants each of its pages to do. The site celebrates the expertise of regular people, whether that expertise is business-related or pertains to a hobby or specialized interest. Squidoo lenses aren't primarily sales tools, and too heavy of a sales emphasis will get you in trouble with the site. So will any kind of spamming, so Squidoo is a little more reserved than Facebook or Twitter on that count, but not quite as formal as LinkedIn. You can

contact people you don't know with a personal, relevant comment or
e-mail, but not barrage strangers with sales pitches they don't want
(which you're not supposed to do anywhere). Lenses do offer links
to products for sale, within the context of the content.

One of the great things about Squidoo is how easy the lenses are
to create. In fact, Squidoo encourages experimentation, because it's
always easy to tweak your lens when you think of a better way to
do it. The best lenses are topical rather than focused on a business or
product. How-to is a big draw on Squidoo, and Squidoo pages come
up frequently in Google search results.

Another way Squidoo differs from most other social media sites
is the amount of support available to budding lensmasters. SquidU
is the online learning arm of Squidoo, and it offers virtual classes,
FAQs, and answer banks to help users create and improve their
lenses. You can recommend lenses that you personally find useful
(which creates community goodwill and positive recognition), and
if you build a great lens, you might get recommended by someone
else. (It's not okay to solicit other lensmasters to recommend you,
but you can ask your friends, family, opt-in list, and colleagues to
visit your site and rate/recommend it.)

Squidoo even offers a way to earn royalties on your lenses,
which you can keep or donate to charity. Royalties are a function of
the amount of traffic generated by your lens, and they're made possible by the ads placed by Squidoo on the site.

It's essential with any social media site to read the rules (and
abide by them), and Squidoo makes that very easy with clear guidelines written in everyday language. I've also found Squidoo support
to be very human-centric and responsive. Squidoo also has a vibrant
community of lensmasters who have a culture of helping and giving,
so polite inquiries are likely to get helpful responses.

Anatomy of a Squidoo Lens

~ **Ads.** Squidoo is supported in part by its ad revenues,
and it's those revenues that can pay royalties or chari-
table donations. You'll see ads on some other social
media sites, but they don't share the profit.

- ~ **Profile.** A good profile adds credibility and helps readers who like your lens find your Website. Make sure to take the time to create a good profile.

- ~ **Summary.** Starting the page with a descriptive and appealing title, plus a succinct and compelling summary, is a good way to draw readers who want to access your knowledge.

- ~ **Body.** Squidoo lenses are varied. Many lenses share a long list of links to resources on a particular topic, recommendations of products or sites, movie reviews, and other information. If you're going to do a list lens, consider giving it some interactivity by allowing readers to vote for their favorites or add to the list.

- ~ **Related topics.** Squidoo tries to steer readers toward other lenses that deal with similar topics. That's another reason to make sure your lens is appropriately titled and tagged with good keywords.

- ~ **Recommendations.** As a lensmaster, you can recommend lenses by other people. Those lenses can be related to your topic, or just lenses you liked. Your recommended lenses list becomes a sidebar on your lens.

- ~ **Comments.** Squidoo is a lively community, and readers enjoy making comments. Having a comments area is a good way to get to know other "Squids," as readers and lensmasters are collectively known.

- ~ **Lensroll.** Similar to a blogroll, it's a list of other lenses you enjoy.

- ~ **Related products.** Squidoo has relationships with Google, Amazon, and eBay, making it easy to refer readers to products that are sold on those sites.

- ~ **Add Modules.** You'll find hundreds of modules to add to your lens, with more added all the time.

- ~ **Health.** This tab lets you know what you need to add to improve your lens, and does it in such a friendly way you don't mind.

- ~ **Lens Stats.** This gives you a snapshot of how much the lens has earned and how it's been rated.

Other ways to organize your page: Squidoo lenses with clear organization, graphics that enhance rather than detract, links to quality resources, and good information tend to do well with ratings and recommendations. One of Squidoo's strengths is its flexibility, so before you create a lens, browse some of the Top 100 lenses, both those that are related to your topic, and some completely outside your industry. You'll see layouts that work well, and some that are not as appealing. You can add YouTube video, links to blog posts and articles, and step-by-step instructions for a process, or have your blog feed your lens via RSS.

Creating Your Squidoo Lens

Squidoo is one of the most helpful sites you'll find on the Internet. Its lens creation process is extremely easy. The emphasis is on enjoying what you're doing as well as creating a way to share what you love with other readers. Squidoo takes passion very seriously, and so do its readers. Kick off your shoes and write from the heart, and your lens will connect with readers. Be informative, be helpful, and, above all, be conversational.

When you begin your page, you'll be asked to create a title, supply relevant keywords, and make a few other easy choices. Then you'll enter the lens workshop area, which makes it easy to add copy or photos, or to include information from Amazon, Flickr, eBay, and other sites. The page is set up in modules, which you can drag and drop to put in any order you want, but you're not limited by just the modules that are initially listed on the blank site.

You can also adjust the settings on the lens and add keyword tags. If you get stuck, Squidoo has fantastic resources to help, including the SquidU Review, a lively discussion forum, and the Answer Deck. The Answer Deck is especially good for first-time Squids, because it lists the most frequently asked questions and answers. Squidoo also offers two free e-books to make the lens creation process easier. One great way to plan your lens is to see what others have created in your topic and then look for gaps you can fill or new information you can provide. Checking out the Lens of the Day is fun because you never know what you'll find.

Using Squidoo for Business

Squidoo invites you to take a back-door approach to promotion rather than charging in through the front gate. At a time when the Internet seems to be full of blaring sites that hawk merchandise and offer endless "squeeze" pages hammering on the reader to buy, Squidoo returns to the original (and best) sales platform: having something valuable to say that solves a problem.

Good Squidoo lenses are simple. Write from your passion. Share information that actually helps someone solve a problem or that provides content that's perfect for a fellow fan of your favorite topic. Try to make your lens as useful and easy to read as you can. If you provide good content, the community rewards you by viewing your lens and making positive comments and recommendations. So avoid blatant sales pitches and the hard sell. Make the lens about your product, not about you or your company. And if your first draft of a lens isn't perfect, don't worry about it. Get some new ideas, read the Squidoo e-books for inspiration, and do better next time.

With that said, here are some ways you can live within the culture of Squidoo and still have your business benefit from one or more lenses:

~ Create lenses by topic. Instead of creating a lens for your business as a whole, write a helpful "how-to" lens on each of the different areas of knowledge that have contributed to your success. (Don't worry; you won't give away all your secrets.) You can start with the kind of information you'd use for an article or blog post, but then add features with Squidoo modules to make that information even more useful.

~ Focus on solving a problem. This is another type of how-to lens, focused on a problem instead of a topic. Again, the magic is in making the lens as useful a resource as possible without turning it into a sales pitch. Don't make the lens all about you and your company and your solution. Approach the topic fresh, with plenty of links to resources, including your own.

~ Indulge your passion. People who have a passion, whether it's for building model airplanes or building businesses, often love to share their knowledge with others. Write a lens on something you're passionately interested in, even if it doesn't have a direct link to your products/services. Your bio will let people who like your lens find out more about you.

~ Promote your book with free sample copy, links to on-line bookstores, a list of reviewers or bloggers who have mentioned your book, and some of the nitty-gritty details you didn't get a chance to share in the book. Make it fun, make it personal, and make it valuable.

~ Show readers how to get more out of a product or service they already use. Maybe it's your product, or maybe you have a related add-on to extend functionality. Create a site that shows readers how to do more with less, stretch a dollar, save money, or get more bang for their buck, and you'll do well.

~ Promote your podcast or blog. You can use RSS to embed your podcast or blog feed, and use Squidoo's easy-to-build lens to make a great homepage at a fraction of the cost of most custom Websites. You can also promote your eBay site, or create a virtual online store focused just on products related to your topic.

~ Share information other "topic nerds" will love. Have you ever heard a group of people who all share the love of an arcane subject talk when it's just among themselves? The joy of sharing minutia with other people who really appreciate it is tremendously rewarding, whatever your interest is. Squidoo lenses are the perfect place to share all that wonderful information that makes your friends' eyes glaze over but will be appreciated by fellow enthusiasts, and to find people who love those details as much as you do. A great lens that goes deep into a topic can give you subject-matter expertise and credibility among the Squidoo readership, and that can lead to a guest blog or speaking invitations, or just great traffic!

Results Reminder

Passion and helpfulness are the keys to success on Squidoo.

The Rule of 30

Take 30 minutes to put your first draft Squidoo page together, and have fun adding to it.

Exercises

1. Experiment with building a Squidoo lens. Draw on links and content you already have, look at what other sites on the topic are doing, and then offer something new.

2. Explore Squidoo to get a feel for trends, and pay attention to Squidoo's unique culture.

3. Enjoy the process of putting a lens together and then returning for 30 minute "spruce-up" sessions when you find new resources to add to your lens.

4. Add a new lens whenever you have something to say about trends or headlines, when you launch a new book or product, or when you discover a hunger in the marketplace for information you can share.

14 Can You Digg It?

If you've ever dog-eared a page in a magazine or put a sticky note on a newspaper article to flag it for someone else's attention, you already understand the premise behind social bookmarking sites like Digg, Delicious, and StumbleUpon.

Social bookmarking sites make it possible to share with the world links to articles and online content (videos, photos, audio, etc.) that you find interesting. It works like your Web browser's bookmark function, saving your favorite links, but it shares those favorites with everyone, who then get to vote on whether or not they find the link interesting, and provide suggestions of their own. (That's the "social" part.)

Social bookmarking sites also serve as a human-driven filter. Many Internet users suffer from information overload just looking at the millions of Google results an average search can create. Sites like Digg, Delicious, and StumbleUpon enable users to categorize their favorite types of information, and then view top links that have been recommended by people, not machines, based on relevancy and content. It's not that different from choosing the next book you read based on the *New York Times* Bestseller list, or looking at the top-selling songs on iTunes before making a purchase.

Social bookmarking is based on the premise that despite the clutter and overload on the Internet, good content will rise to the top because of word of mouth. Sites such as Digg and the others centralize word of mouth and have created systems to share, vote on, and link to what their user base considers to be the best content on the Web. The sites vary in how they rate and recommend content, but, in general, the goal is to send you content that is matched to the preferences you've specified and either your friends' choices or the choices of people with similar profiles and preferences (similar to the recommendations Amazon makes of books other readers also bought when they purchased the book you buy).

On social bookmarking sites, the conversation is all about content. You share your favorites, comment and vote on what others share, and invite your friends to see what you're sharing.

Anatomy of a Social Bookmarking Site

Although each of the sites is a little different, let's take a look at Digg to get an idea of what your social bookmarking site might look like.

~ **Profile.** Once again, the most important part of your site, because it lets people get to know you. Post a photo, tell the world a little bit about you (focus on the professional because you're using Digg for business), and show some personality.

~ **Favorites.** When you read an item on Digg, you can vote on its usefulness (Digg or Bury), reTweet it on Twitter, send it to your Facebook site, or e-mail it to a friend. If you really love an article, you can add it to your favorites, where others can see what you like.

~ **Add friends.** Depending on your e-mail browser, you can either import your friends' contact information or invite people one by one. When you add friends, you'll be able to see their favorites as well.

~ **Best of Digg.** Subscribe to Digg's RSS feed and get daily or weekly updates on what's hot on Digg. Great for trend-watching.

~ **Customize.** This lets you filter which topics you see so that your information is streamlined.

~ **Submit new.** Upload your own items to Digg, either links to things you've written or links to interesting items by someone else.

Using Social Bookmarking for Business

Although social bookmarking sites focus on content more than on amassing huge followings of friends, sites such as Digg, Delicious, and StumbleUpon can be very helpful to your business in several ways. They allow you to:

~ Stay informed. Part of being an expert is earning a reputation of being the "go-to" person for information on your topic. Experts have to constantly take in new information to stay relevant, and social bookmarking sites make it easier to scan topics in your industry.

~ Add and share links. Social bookmarking sites make it easy to share links via your other social media sites, and to find good links to share in blogs and newsletters. When you refer readers to resources beyond what you create yourself, you build a reputation as a trend-leader and guru.

~ Share your own links with the world. Upload links to your blog posts, podcasts, Tweets, individual Webpages, online articles, and press releases with other readers and help your content go viral.

~ Watch trends: Keeping an eye on the top trends and watching to see which items get the most buzz can help you shape your own marketing topics and tap into the hottest subjects.

~ Do a favor: Share your friends' and colleagues' articles, Tweets, reviews, and blog posts, and post positive comments to generate buzz.

~ Connect with other readers: When you comment on articles and respond to comment threads, you'll get to know some of the most active users on that site. Many users have links to their Facebook or Twitter sites, where you can friend or follow them to continue the conversation.

~ Encourage your readers to pass along and bookmark your blog posts, podcasts, videos, and Webpages by using the icon buttons from AddThis.com. The buttons make it easy for anyone to forward the content so your work gets a wider readership.

~ Demonstrate your expertise by forwarding consistently good, thought-provoking links to articles about your topic or industry, and by making thoughtful, intelligent comments on links posted by others.

~ Blog about links you find on social bookmarking sites, and send a link of your blog post to the person who originally posted the interesting content.

Results Reminder

Building expert credibility is a long-term process enhanced one link, blog, or comment at a time.

The Rule of 30

How quickly can you find 30 valuable pieces of information to add to your social bookmarking site?

30

Exercises

1. Open an account and complete your profile on at least one social bookmarking site.

2. Fill out your preferences so you begin to get link referrals. Check out the information and see what people are talking about that relates to your topic.

3. Watch for trends that relate to your expertise. It's a great way to find headlines that get attention.

4. Find 30 articles, blog posts, videos, audios, or Websites that you think are interesting enough to bookmark (these can be your own or links to valuable content by other people) and add them to your site.

5. Watch how the conversation develops. Learn and repeat.

YouTube and Flickr: Your Windows to the World

15

If your idea of sharing videos is sitting through an interminable travelogue as a child, think again. Today's online video world is funny, irreverent, home-grown, surprisingly professional, and powerfully viral.

YouTube is still the granddaddy of video-sharing sites. YouTube makes it very easy to upload, tag, describe, and share your videos, and to find, watch, and comment on videos by other people. It's surprisingly addictive, whether you're surfing for business or pleasure, and many homemade videos get viewership some TV shows only dream of receiving.

Flickr is a top photo-sharing site. Though some people use Flickr to share photos from vacations and pictures of smiling babies, there are lots of ways Flickr can help you add visuals to your social media sites to make them more lively and interesting.

Digital videography and photography has made both YouTube and Flickr possible. To get started, try purchasing an inexpensive digital video camera that has the ability to easily upload video to a computer. A great option is the Flip video camera that has a built-in USB connector and plugs right into of your computer, but you can use most newer digital video cameras with a little extra effort. For Flickr, any digital camera that can upload via a USB cable is good to get you started.

Today's consumers expect a multimedia experience from their Web-browsing time. Video and photos make your sites more interesting, more personal, and less static. Prospects get to feel as if they know you better by watching short video clips that feature you sharing information in an entertaining way. Video and photos are a great way to let your personality shine through in an otherwise impersonal medium.

One important difference between YouTube and Flickr is that YouTube has embraced business users and business content, and Flickr does not allow commercial use. That's an important difference, and one you'll need to keep in mind. (That's why it's so important to read the terms and rules for yourself.) What that means is that while it's okay to upload videos on YouTube that have business content, share a how-to about a product or service, or give a soft promotion of your company, it's not okay on Flickr to upload logos, product photos, or advertisements. There are ways you can still use Flickr to add personality and interest to your social media sites without violating their rules, so keep reading.

Anatomy of a YouTube page

~ **Find Friends.** YouTube is part of social media, and inviting everyone you know to your new account is just being sociable. You can import friends from your e-mail account, let your Facebook and Twitter friends know about your new YouTube channel, and search for people you know one at a time. Get to know the community before you invite strangers.

~ **Subscriptions.** When you find YouTube content that you think is helpful, interesting, or useful, you can subscribe to that user's RSS feed. Remember to use social bookmarking to let others know when you've found a gem. The Subscriptions section will cluster your favorite channels and their newest videos, to keep you from having to go looking for them.

~ **Recommended for You.** Based on what you've shown that you like, YouTube makes suggestions of other videos you might enjoy. It's a great way to find new and valuable information.

~ **Inbox.** Once you begin uploading and subscribing to videos, you'll begin to hear from the community through personal messages, comments, friend invitations, and other messages. You can also use messaging to reach out to people who have posted content you enjoy, which is the best way to make new YouTube friends.

~ **Recent Activity.** This module lets you see all the new content your friends have recently added, even if you don't subscribe to their channel. It also shows you their newest favorites and video ratings. (Hint: Everything you do is also visible to everyone else, so be warned.)

~ **Featured Videos.** YouTube picks its own favorites and lets you know about it.

~ **Videos Being Watched Now.** A great way to see what's trending and what's hot.

~ **YouTube blog.** The best way to pick up hints, tips, and news to become a power user.

~ **Account Settings.** Lets you customize the modules on your home page, set up your profile, create a blog, and manage your privacy and e-mail.

Anatomy of a Flickr Page

~ **Personalize Your Profile.** Add a photo of yourself and a bio that focuses on personal (not business) identity. Remember: Flickr doesn't like commercial use, and you don't want to get warned or blocked.

~ **Upload Your Photos.** Transfer your photos to your computer from your digital camera. Flickr also accepts videos up to 90 seconds in length. Make sure you tag and describe your photos with good keywords and interesting captions. Don't forget to use the RSS icons to share your new photos with all your other social media sites and to add them to the social bookmarking sites too.

~ **Find Friends.** Invite your e-mail list and your other social media friends to join you on Flickr. Tread carefully when making new friends, and base your introductions on the quality of content and a meaningful comment about their photos. Make quality connections and don't spam. It's not about quantity. Remember to keep it personal and don't even think of selling.

~ **Your Photostream.** When you upload photos, your photos appear in this section.

~ **Explore.** This is the fun part. It's like flipping through the world's collective photo albums. You'll find everything and anything. It can be addictive!

~ **Flickr Blog.** A great way to find new content, see what others are doing, and learn more about the community.

Using YouTube and Flickr for Business

~ Use your digital video camera to record short (less than 5 minutes) video segments where you give an entertaining "how-to" on something in your area of expertise. You can also do a short commentary on a headline topic, share a few tips, or create a funny but meaningful short commercial. Use your imagination.

~ Set up your own YouTube channel through regular video posts. You could record tips, interview other business or thought leaders, or chop up your webinars into small segments to share.

~ Add your YouTube videos to your homepage, or stream them with RSS to your podcast, blog, or other social media sites such as Facebook.

~ Use social bookmarking to let everyone know when you've uploaded new video.

~ Tweet about your new YouTube videos and get feedback.

~ Look for others doing interesting business videos and reach out to them. Tweet and bookmark their videos. Provide positive and helpful comments. Connect outside of YouTube through Facebook or e-mail. Invite them to be your YouTube friends.

~ Encourage your friends, followers, and e-mail list to forward your videos and share them.

~ Embed a link to your newest video in your e-mail newsletter, or put a link to a particularly good video in your e-mail signature block.

~ Create a specially themed YouTube video series and then blog about it. Announce the series premier via press releases, and set up an episode guide. Herald the last episode of the season, and host an online or real wrap party for friends and followers.

~ Repurpose webinars and speaking videos (ones for which you own the copyright) by chopping them into short segments and posting them as a series with new introduction/ending slides.

~ Encourage your clients and purchasers to create and up-load videos of themselves using your product, and run a contest for the best video.

~ When you travel for business, create a video blog of the activity, and take viewers along for the ride. (Always ask permission before including anyone else on your video blog, make sure everyone looks professional, and don't share anything that might embarrass anyone or infringe on someone else's copyright.)

~ Because Flickr doesn't want commercial content, you'll need to tread carefully. But you're a business *person*, so your photos can focus on the personality side of your experience.

~ Heading to a conference in an interesting location? Snap some photos of the scenery and upload them to Flickr, then share them on your social media sites.

~ Having fun at a trade show or event? Share photos of yourself with friends and colleagues. (Always ask permission first and make sure everyone looks their best.)

~ Encourage your friends to take your book or product on vacation with them and send you video or photos of them with your book or product in exotic locales. Create a scrapbook of their travels.

~ Snap a photo of yourself in front of your store when it's decorated for the holidays.

~ When you speak, win an award, or are otherwise featured, upload the photo with an appropriate caption.

~ Throw in some fun personal photos: your pet, a few vacation scenery shots, and the like. It's okay to have a life. If you have a creative talent and want to showcase some artistic photography, create a folder and have fun! Prospects want to know that you're a real person. (Note: Use caution when sharing anything that might be misinterpreted, and, as a general rule, avoid sharing photos of your children, home, or other highly personal settings.)

~ Make sure you tag and caption your Flickr photos to make them useful and meaningful, and then use RSS to automatically send your new photos to your social media sites.

~ Look for photos you enjoy on Flickr, and add useful and positive comments, join in the discussion, bookmark and Tweet about your finds, and get to know other users. Although Flickr doesn't endorse mass friending or business promotion, when you get out and just meet people without an agenda or a time line, you'll be amazed how you're drawn to like-minded people with shared interests.

Results Reminder

A picture is worth a thousand words—and it helps to personalize your social media sites!

The Rule of 30

How could you share your year in 30 photos?

30

Exercises

1. Make a list of events of which you'll attend or speak. Plan to snap 30 digital photos with captions that are fun and showcase your business travel or activities.

2. Encourage your clients to send you digital photos of themselves wearing/using your product (or carrying it to exotic locations). Recognize submissions in your newsletter.

Get Business From Forums, Chats, and Threads

16

When the Internet first began, it was heavily populated with people from academic backgrounds who recognized its early potential as a place to share resources and trade information. Although the Internet has become heavily commercialized since those early days, that culture of giving still strongly dominates what citizens of the Net consider to be appropriate community behavior. It's not really different from off-line community behavior in that we like to get to know people before they try to sell us something. One of the best online opportunities to show that you're a good Net neighbor and a credible expert is through the forums, chats, and discussion threads that pertain to your topic or industry.

The Power of Answering Questions

Many sites devoted to a topic, hobby, industry, or special interest have places to ask and answer questions. To reduce spam, most of these areas require either membership or a log-in registration. Choose your registration name carefully, because when you're on the Internet to grow your business, you want people to easily identify you so they can find your Website, company, or products. It's best to choose the closest user name to your real name or your company's name possible, and avoid extra numbers or symbols that might make it difficult to remember.

Once you're logged in, spend some time browsing before you begin answering or asking questions. Get a feel for who the regulars are and what the tone of the site is. Can you spot particular trends in topics? Do a few people dominate the conversation? Are there many new people looking for information or is it just a private venting space between a few old hands?

Ideally, you're looking for a vibrant discussion area where there is a good mix between experts, new users, and returning questioners. Healthy sites have a broad variety of contributors, not just a few dominant voices, and maintain a welcoming attitude toward a diversity of opinions.

Your goal is to find a few sites where you can become a trusted and valued member of the community by providing quality answers to meaningful questions that pertain to your area of expertise. For example, the forum at MarketingProfs.com is alive with different conversations, and it welcomes experts, students, and business owners to the lively discussion on marketing issues. Some sites (such as MarketingProfs.com) even award points for the best answers, creating a competition among experts to provide the most useful information in exchange for the honor of becoming a contributor with a lot of points.

Whether or not the site provides a ranking system, it won't take long for you to figure out who provides the best information and who is looked to for leadership and sound advice within the site's culture. Becoming a recognized expert on a site isn't a quick-results marketing tactic, but it can pay off in the future as online admirers begin to seek you out for consulting or collaboration projects.

Chats, Forums, and Threads

Discussion sites tend to have three main structures: chats, forums, or threads. Each works a little differently, but they can all be valid ways to demonstrate your expertise within a community that has value to you.

Chats occur in real time, similar to instant messaging or cell phone texts, but in a chat room. Everyone logged into the room can read the conversation. People either meet up spontaneously or agree to meet for a pre-scheduled event, and then discuss a topic. Questions and answers happen live, and a record of the chat conversation can be saved or printed for archiving.

Forums are the most common, and they consist of a posted question and then answers contributed by any member who chooses to reply. Forums are an online circle where someone can seek the insight of the larger group, usually to solve a problem or find a particular resource. There can be a time lag of hours or days between when the question posts and when answers appear, and some forum conversations can go on indefinitely. Forum posts can also be archived, saved, or printed.

Threads are more like e-mails with a long history of replies and forwards. Often, they begin as emails that are publicly readable, with many people jumping in to add their input. They can stay focused on the original topic, or veer onto tangential matters. Comment sections on blogs fall into the threads category. As with chats and forums, thread content lasts essentially forever and can be printed or saved.

The benefit of responding to chats, forums, and threads is that you can achieve global visibility for the price of some good answers. Most questions take only about 15 minutes for a thoughtful reply. If you sign your posts with a signature block that includes your name, Website and company, readers who like what you have to say can find you outside of the site for further conversation. (Avoid including an e-mail address to keep robo-spammers from harvesting your information.)

The reality is that only about 10 percent of a site's members participate actively in creating or maintaining content. Most members just browse a site, or drop in from time to time. If you're willing to be consistent with your posts and you share good information, you can gain a reputation as a go-to expert within a few months.

Make Comments Work Harder for You

You can repurpose the great content you share in chats, threads, comments, and forums in several ways so that you write once and reap the benefit over and over. If the site offers social bookmarking, use those links to let the world know about the exciting conversation you're having. (Many membership sites are password protected and don't offer this feature, but some public sites do.) Additionally, many membership sites have "badges" with the site logo and a link to your profile, which may include your recent posts. Use this to connect your other Websites and social media pages and invite others to join in the discussion.

Save a copy of your posts and reuse them in your blog with a re-stated question, or use the short forum answer as the jumping off point for a longer article, blog post, Twitter series, or as fodder for a future book. Spot trends and hot topics by watching the most lively discussions, and then maximize that trendiness by talking about that topic at more length on your Twitter or blog, or by inviting your social media friends/followers to a whole new discussion on your own sites.

You can also post questions of your own on chat/forum/thread sites, and invite feedback, case studies, and the perspective of other site members. This can be very valuable for developing material for articles and speeches, or for tweaking presentations with real-life examples.

Words to the Wise: Be Careful Out There

As with anything else on the Internet, what you post on a chat, forum, comment, or thread lasts forever and is potentially searchable. It's advisable to think before you post, and to avoid commenting when you're angry or in a bad mood. Remember that a topic about which you feel passionate today might seem unimportant next year, but your comments, if intemperate, can dog you forever. Make sure everything you post shows you in your best light as a credible, even-tempered, level-headed expert people who would trust with their business.

Remember that slander and libel laws still pertain to online copy, and avoid posting information to harm anyone's reputation. Likewise, plagiarism and copyright infringement rules also apply to forum/chat/thread posts, so make sure that your content is original or that you attribute quotes from others appropriately. It's considered a breech of etiquette to quote someone outside of the forum discussion without their permission (and on some sites, doing so will terminate your account). If tempers flare, take the high road and maintain professional decorum.

Always read over your post before submitting to check for tone and spelling. Make sure that your post can't be easily misconstrued or taken out of context, and that your tone remains friendly. Avoid sarcasm, as it doesn't translate well for non-native speakers and can lead to misunderstandings. Most sites have a zero-tolerance policy for spamming other members or making hard-sell sales pitches, so know and respect the rules for the community.

You can make a good start at becoming an expert in a chat/forum/thread in 30 days, but realize that relationships require time to deepen, and your continued, consistent participation will be what ultimately leads to business connections.

Results Reminder

Becoming the go-to expert of the online forum requires commitment, but it pays off in global recognition and opportunities for new business.

The Rule of 30

Thirty posts during 30 days read by 30 people gives you exposure to 900 people you wouldn't have met.

30

Exercises

1. Sign up for one or two membership sites that are relevant to your business that have online forums (check to see how lively the forums are before joining).

2. Each day for 30 days, answer at least one question. Make sure you have a good signature block and provide helpful content.

3. Use the online profiles to get to know your fellow experts and the frequent questioners. Think about how to add value and extend the conversation.

Raise the ROI From Your Interest and Industry Sites

17

Some of the richest opportunities in social media marketing are also among the most overlooked. Almost every organization now offers an online community as part of its membership, but few people take full advantage of the opportunities this creates to do business with a larger marketplace. Alumni organizations; chambers of commerce; business, professional and industry clubs; and trade associations all offer fantastic possibilities to meet prospects, find collaborators and joint venture partners, and increase sales.

Start With the Profile

Your profile is the way others will get their first glimpse of who you are and what expertise you offer. Start with a current photo. Without a photo, your profile has no face. People want to deal with other people, and your photo assures readers that you are a real person.

Some sites have profiles that focus on academic or career milestones, whereas others offer more freedom with bulleted lists or paragraphs. Make your profile compelling with a focus on the benefit you offer to clients and the problem you solve. Incorporate links to audio or video to let your personality shine through. Keep paragraphs short and use active verbs.

Remember that a profile isn't supposed to be a resume. Keep it conversational and benefit-oriented, but add enough career details to underscore your credibility. If you've published, add the titles of your most recent books. If the profile asks for hobby information, pick a few favorites; these can be great ice-breakers for conversation and may attract fellow hobbyists. Details like hobbies also help to humanize your profile and provide a sense of personality.

Get More From the Directory

Club, organization, or association sites often list an online membership directory. Used correctly, this can be a powerful tool to make profitable new connections. Shared membership does not make it okay to spam others, and unsolicited sales pitches can lead to revoked privileges or banishment from the site. Instead, look for real areas of common interest with individuals, and send a personal e-mail to introduce yourself and set up a phone call. Indicate what you'd like to discuss, to allay any fears that your call might become a sales pitch. Good reasons to connect include the possibility of collaboration or joint venture, the opportunity to share resources or become referral sources for each other, or the chance to become allies in winning new business.

Make your initial e-mail personal, friendly, and brief. Don't include a lot of links and don't try to sell anything. Introduce yourself as a fellow member, and mention what it was about that person's profile that intrigued you. Suggest a way you might be able to help each other, and ask to set up a phone call. Use the call to determine how good a fit there is in interest and personality, and go from there. Because most members completely ignore the potential connections in the membership database, you'll probably be one of a very few who make the effort to get to know members outside the local area.

Through the membership database, other new opportunities can appear. For example, by getting to know someone in your organization who lives in a different state or country, you might be invited to speak at their chapter's meeting or submit a blog post, article, or white paper. Striking up professional friendships across the country or around the world makes it easy to ask for an insider's perspective when travel takes you to your acquaintance's home territory. Buying decisions in a global, Internet economy are no longer based on proximity, and your new contacts may be able to help you save costs or increase productivity by suggesting resources you hadn't discovered.

Don't rule out connecting with other firms that appear to be competitors. Few companies are really identical in skills or emphasis, and, often, erstwhile competitors can win more or larger contracts by allying, leveraging their particular strengths.

If your organization has an annual conference, use the membership database to help you schedule meetings with high-potential prospects before you ever leave home. A couple of months before the conference, contact the people you're most interested in getting to know to see if they plan to attend. If so, make arrangements to meet for breakfast, lunch, or a late cocktail. Instead of wondering whether or not the trip will be productive, you'll have a slate of scheduled meetings set up before you go.

Don't forget that clubs, associations, and organizations often have affiliate members that are vendors who provide services or offer discounts to club members. You can use the site's social media tools to get to know these affiliate members as well, and use the same strategies to reach out to them for networking or in preparation for attending a conference or trade show. Vendors can be powerful referral sources as well as valuable partners. Creating a connection through the social media tools on a membership site can eliminate the awkwardness of a sales call by first building a relationship based on shared interests. If the site posts the show program in advance, check out the speakers, breakout leaders, and key vendors you'd most like to meet, and see if they're listed in the membership directory. If so, make a pre-show connection and arrange your meeting ahead of time. This is a great way to stand out from the crowd because at the show, you won't be making an introduction: you'll be renewing an existing acquaintance.

You can also use the membership directory to get to know the chapter leaders in other cities or regions. This can open doors for speaking engagements, guest blogging, or new networking opportunities. When you are planning to travel to an area with a chapter of your organization, use the membership directory to touch base with local members to meet for coffee or dinner. Join the sub-groups for your organization or club on other social media sites, such as Facebook or LinkedIn, and get to know members in other areas through the chats and forums. You'll be amazed how that online relationship can accelerate the formation of alliances and profitable opportunities when you finally meet in person.

Take a Leadership Role

The social media tools of club, association, organization, and alumni sites are powerful because of shared allegiance as well as shared interests and common goals. Compared to the gigantic size of public sites such as Facebook, most club or industry sites are relatively small communities within which it's easier to get to know people and to make a name for yourself as a helpful expert. Because most sites and communities rely on a small percentage of active members to generate content and keep the site functioning, you can become a leader by something as simple as showing up frequently with consistently good contributions and a genuine interest in helping all the members grow and succeed.

The advice in Chapter 16 about posting helpful answers and good questions in chat/forum/thread/comment sections also holds true on the club and association sites. You may also be able to post to a member blog, or contribute content to a shared blog. Show leadership qualities by staying out of online arguments and offering solidly good information based on your area of expertise. Reference your company, experience, or products, but don't do a hard sell. Offer to lead special discussions, moderate forums, or organize online events. Work with the site moderator to create polls or member surveys, and then share the results with the group. You'll be visible in a very positive way, and members will get to recognize your name and company.

If your content is firmly rooted in your expertise and sprinkled with client examples and mini case studies, members will get a clear idea of what you offer and the solutions you provide without the need for you to resort to actual selling. A good profile and signature block for your forum posts will make it easy for interested readers to contact out outside of the site if they are interested in your services.

Results Reminder

Lead by giving great information and by helping others succeed to achieve prominence in any online membership community.

The Rule of 30

Meet 30 new people from the database, post 30 answers to forum questions, or arrange calls or meetings with 30 other members and watch opportunity blossom!

30

Exercises

1. Create a complete and compelling profile that focuses on the benefit you provide to clients and the problems you solve.

2. Apply the knowledge of your best client/prospect/partner that you gained from reviewing profiles in the member database, and craft a personal, customized introductory e-mail that emphasizes connection, not sales.

3. Leverage your membership by looking for groups related to the club/organization on Facebook, LinkedIn, and Twitter.

18 ◁ Social Media and PR

Social media has blurred the lines between public relations (PR) and online marketing. It's also created a powerful tool for business owners, professionals, and authors to reach global audiences and create "viral" buzz in ways that could only be dreamed about by the large advertising agencies of past decades. Though there are some ways in which PR and social media can reinforce each other, there are also distinct differences, and a wise self-promoter will respect the distinctions.

A Quick PR Primer

Public relations is the art of getting free publicity, usually through coverage in traditional media such as newspapers, magazines, TV, and radio. With the growth of the Internet, that field of possibilities has expanded to include the online versions of newspapers and magazines, video sites like YouTube, and both podcasts and online radio shows like those offered by Blog Talk Radio.

The workhorse of traditional PR is the press release, which even in the Internet age remains much the same. The standard format looks like this:

FOR IMMEDIATE RELEASE

CONTACT: (Your name and e-mail or phone here)
Catchy Headline With Good Keywords

City, State: Compelling first sentence with top key-words and action verbs and one or two more short sentences that cover who, what, when, where, and why we should care.

Second short paragraph (one to three sentences) that provides background and context.

Third short paragraph (one to three sentences) that includes a one-line recap of your company and what it does and for whom, plus e-mail, Website, and phone number.

That's it—nothing mysterious or esoteric about it, but that deceptively simple document will showcase your skill in making editors and readers care about what you're offering.

One of the biggest changes the Internet has made to public relations is the ability for regular folks who aren't reporters to find their own news online without the media middlemen. Most people today will run a Google search on a topic rather than wait for tomorrow's newspaper, next month's magazine, or the 6 o'clock evening news. Online news sites operate 24/7, creating an insatiable demand for news that relies on a steady stream of good story leads from publicists and press releases. On one hand, that means your news has never been needed as much by news sites as it is today. On the other hand, it means there is an incredible amount of clutter your release must rise above in order to be noticed.

The Many New Faces of News

Pre-Internet, it was easy to find reporters because they worked for newspapers, magazines, TV, or radio. Today, blogs and social media sites have created the rise of the citizen journalist, people who report or comment on topics without formal training or a job with a media outlet. Some sites are private rants; others show good reportorial skill and a true newshound's nose for a story. In recent years, bloggers have broken major stories before long-established newspapers.

News outlets (for example, CNN) have begun to embrace and cultivate the citizen journalist by providing ways for people to upload their own on-the-scene videos, cell phone photos, and reports. The ability to text, Tweet, and photograph via cell phone from a scene with breaking news means that the average person who is in the right place at the right time stands a good chance of being the lead story on the news. The rise of the citizen journalist coupled with decreasing ad revenue and declining subscriptions has led to the surviving newspapers and magazines cutting back on some sections of coverage. Book reviews are a good example of this trend, and a place where social media sites have more than filled the gap, providing more outlets for coverage than ever before.

Is It News or Social Media?

The answer: both. Social media is just a new vehicle for the oldest form of news: word of mouth. The difference lies in the style of the communication and the relationship with the audience. Although their influence has waned, traditional news outlets remain important for publicity-seekers. But where it used to require mailing, e-mailing, or calling a reporter, now it's possible to find a reporter's social media sites and strike up a conversation in a less formal and more accessible setting. Reporters and hosts of radio and TV programs now blog, Tweet, and post Facebook pages, all of which make it possible to comment or connect outside of traditional channels. The key difference is that connections made via social media should be conversational, whereas the real pitch should be made via traditional channels such as e-mail or phone.

Today's corporate press pages often include blogs, Twitter feeds, YouTube videos, and audio, and offer reporters the chance to subscribe via an RSS feed. You can create a similar one-stop media (and consumer) page on your Website and incorporate your social media sites to provide a content-rich introduction to you and your products or services.

Online press-release distribution sites (whether they are pay-for-placement or free posting) are a great way to increase traffic to both your Website and your social media sites. The last paragraph of a press release is called the "boilerplate"; it's copy that stays the same from release to release, and it includes a brief company description and your contact information. When you write releases that are designed to catch the interest of both reporters and consumers, you can steer them to visit your other sites for more information or for immediate sales. Press releases that you post online do two very valuable things: they increase your brand's search engine visibility, and they improve your site's rankings through increased traffic and in-bound links.

The biggest difference between news and social media is in the context and style of the communication. Most newspapers and magazines (whether online or traditional paper) write in a third-person narrative form. This is ideal for the traditional press release. Social media sites, however, are conversational and informal. As a general rule, bloggers and social media site owners don't appreciate getting press releases. They would rather be approached with a personal e-mail or a direct message and a conversational inquiry to see whether the topic would be of interest. News sites tend to cover events, products, and announcements in a detached, impersonal style, which is ideally as unbiased as possible. Social media sites revel in their quirky personality and imbue everything with the voice and perspective of the site owner. Traditional news sites also tend to show more restraint in terms of emotion and avoid the use of profanity. Social media sites are wide-open forums that can range from restrained to no-holds-barred.

When a story, image, or video goes "viral," it means that it so captures the imagination that people begin to send it to their friends without prompting. Sometimes, a viral story or image will also make it into the traditional news if it gains enough popularity. It's important to remember that all PR, viral or not, occurs with a complete lack of control on the part of the originator after the "send" button has been pressed. You may not like what a reporter or blogger says about your company or your product, and you may not approve of the contexts in which your viral image or story is relayed. Too bad. That's how the game is played.

Leveraging PR and Social Media

When you use traditional PR and social media to reinforce each other, utilizing the unique strengths of both vehicles, your publicity can take a huge step forward.

Before you pitch a reporter, check out his or her social media sites. Make thoughtful comments that include a good signature block and reference your company/product/book in a non-sales way. If there are a few key reporters you want to target, you can begin this process long before your release is ready to go live.

Create a blog just for your press releases, and use RSS to feed it to your Website and social media pages so that your news is both easily updated and archived. A news blog also provides the option for interested reporters or citizen journalists to subscribe for future updates. Remember to include your videos and audios as well as your standard press releases.

When you post a press release to an online distribution site, make sure the headlines and copy are keyword-rich for optimum searchability, and have good links to your Website and social media pages. Take readers directly to the appropriate page for the topic, not just to the homepage of your site. Don't forget to fill in the "tags" section, where you can increase searchability even further. When your press release posts online, be sure to add it to the social bookmarking sites for increased visibility.

When you have an article, radio interview, or guest blog posted online, Tweet the link and let your Facebook and LinkedIn friends know by updating your "status" line. Blog about the experience of being interviewed, or augment the article or interview with additional information you didn't have a chance to share and be sure to include the link. Add the link to your online press kit with a tag that shows the name of the publication/blog/station and the date. Be sure to submit the article or interview links to the social bookmarking sites, too.

Create news by blogging live from industry events and creating on-site videos and uploading them. Run polls or surveys on your social media sites, and report the results with a press release to traditional and online news sites. Friend and follow the reporters and bloggers you hope to pitch, and pay attention to the kinds of topics they discuss and cover on their social media sites as well as in their articles, shows, or blogs. Become part of the news by launching your own newsworthy podcast or blog and post solid, non-sales content that attracts the attention of traditional and online media.

Though the lines between news and social media have blurred, consumers benefit from a windfall of information, and companies seeking publicity have more opportunities than ever before. Social media can not only increase the effectiveness of your publicity, but it can create a powerful, interconnected, and global PR platform for you and your business.

Results Reminder

Remember to entertain, inform, and keep the focus of releases on "what's in it for the reader" to get maximum impact.

The Rule of 30

Identify 30 reporters/bloggers/hosts whose show or site is perfect for your audience and topic, then compile their contact information and get started!

30

Exercises

1. Craft your press release with social media and online search in mind, using keywords and short, active sentences.

2. Build your database of online press release distribution sites, traditional and online media, and bloggers and social media sites dedicated to your topic.

3. Make sure your content focuses on the benefit to the reader and remember both reporters and prospective customers will be reading your release.

Social Media and Sales Promotion

19

All sales take place within a community of some kind. That may be a small town, a big city, a region, a country, or the global marketplace, but the community is an essential part of the sales process.

Sales occur because the buyer perceives an urgent need. Sales promotion can't create that need, but it can stoke the sense of urgency, and it can overcome objections by making it easy to buy under very favorable terms.

Social media offers powerful new ways to provide unique promotions to your friends, fans, and followers. You can create special sales or packages just for your social media audience, and get feedback from customers and prospects on what kinds of sales or promotional offers they'd most like to receive. You can also use social media to create incentives for your online friends, fans, and followers to become your virtual sales force and help you spread the word.

The Power of Promotion

Everyone loves to be "in the know." People are attracted by the opportunity to be a VIP and to be inside the inner circle, receiving special benefits not available to everyone. Social media creates a new way to offer coupons, discounts, and advance information on sales and specials to the people who have become your online friends, fans, and followers. By combining the best features of opt-in e-mail marketing and direct response mailings (without the cost of postage), social media promotion can augment your existing promotional strategy and win a loyal following.

One form of social media sales promotion is the rise of Websites (with internal social media components like blogging and Tweeting) that help customers shop for bargains by maximizing their use of coupons. Sites such as TheGroceryGame.com teach shoppers how to get the best value for their grocery dollar while sharing coupons and strategies to reduce costs. These sites create loyal followings and also provide rich territory for marketers to find out sales and product preferences.

If you offer daily or weekly specials, use social media to let your friends and followers know. Tweet about your flavor of the day or about special pricing on limited-quantity items. Blog about upcoming sales with an insider's eye toward getting maximum shopping value. Provide real user benefit by helping shoppers learn how to get better value and stretch their dollars by sharing savvy shopping strategies.

Build on the tried-and-true idea of a VIP membership with social media. Create a Facebook or Twitter page around your VIP specials. Sure, everyone can read the page, but only your VIPs get the specials, creating "results envy" and encouraging non-members to join the club. Or, create your own membership site for your VIPs with a Ning.com site. If you have a VIP area on your Website, add a blog, photos, and Web video. You can even encourage your members to send photos or video of themselves as testimonials.

If you sell from your Website, Tweet, blog, and post to your social media site as soon as new items are uploaded to your online store.

Offer special deals for buyers who shop within the first few hours after a new product is put online. Create early-bird specials that you publicize only on social media to increase the interest in being your social media friend.

Take It to the Street

Radio stations have long used "street teams" of interns or volunteers to post flyers, stuff mailboxes, and raise buzz about upcoming events and new artists. You can create your own street team and leverage the social media power of your most avid online friends and followers by offering them the opportunity to promote a cause or product they believe in.

This works especially well for products that have a highly targeted niche audience, passionate users, and a sense of mission. For example, authors and bands often recruit street teams to help spread the word about a new book or CD. Nonprofits and cause-related organizations frequently recruit street teams in the context of grassroots-level fundraisers, whether they are 5K races, cookie sales, or jump rope marathons.

Street team success requires you to have a highly developed knowledge of your core audience and most devoted fans, and to know what motivates them. Meaningful motivation can be surprisingly inexpensive, and can include recognition, coupons, t-shirts, photos posted online, or the ability to contribute content or input. Authors have sometimes rewarded dedicated street team members by using their name for a character in an upcoming book. Bands give away t-shirts and CDs, or special song or video downloads.

Street teams can be especially effective when their members have credibility within an audience that may be distrustful of traditional advertising or are too small to reach effectively through normal advertising channels. The effectiveness of the street team lies in its members being bona fide members of the target audience or having credibility within the audience as informal leaders and trendsetters. For example, a company selling to college students could recruit street teams from among them who would be able to pass out coupons and promotional items on campus and in dormitories, where traditional advertising might not penetrate. Jewelers or clothing manufacturers who sell to an ethnic minority or recent immigrant audience could leverage the credibility of street team members within these difficult-to-reach audience where relationships and word of mouth have high value.

Social media becomes a key component in keeping touch with your street team members and recruiting new members. It's important to remember that street teamers only participate for as long as being part of the team is fun and personally rewarding. Turnover is high, and street teams should be handled gently to avoid burnout. Always remember that they are doing you a huge favor by passing along your information for free, and treat them graciously. Be lavish with praise, recognition, and whatever freebies you can offer. Make it fun and easy for them to share your message without compromising their credibility or integrity.

With today's growing variety of social media choices, your sales promotion possibilities are limited only by your imagination.

Results Reminder

When you involve customers in creating the promotion, they're eager to pass it along to their friends.

The Rule of 30

Look at your calendar of upcoming promotions. What are 30 ways you could involve your street team or trendsetters/ opinion leaders through social media?

30

Exercises

1. Use StrawPoll, SurveyMonkey.com, Zoomerang.com, or other online survey tools to ask your best customers and prospects who they consider to be trendsetters and opinion leaders. Make a list of potential contacts from their answers.

2. Seek out those leaders on social media and strike up a conversation. Connect and interact before you ask any favors or propose business. Watch what they write about and who is following them.

3. What can you offer in reciprocal benefit to trendsetters/opinion leaders and your street team to keep them interested and active?

20

Social Media for Local Businesses

Now, if you've been thinking that all this social media stuff is too global for a local business, think again. Just as a TV ad campaign can run locally or nationally, a social media campaign can be as large or small in its focus as you design it to be.

Social Media Makes Good Neighbors

Whether you own your own company or operate a local franchise of a national firm, being a good neighbor is essential to creating a successful business. In the past, businesses have demonstrated their neighborliness by being prominent in the local scene. Sponsoring the town's intramural or kids' sports teams; underwriting local pageants, festivals, and holiday celebrations; providing hometown scholarships; and encouraging employees to take visible roles in charity events have all been ways companies have shown themselves to be good neighbors.

Being neighborly also includes creating a sense of community by hosting programs that offer a chance for local people to mingle, relax, and get to know each other. Some examples might include a health workshop held by a local medical practice; live music at a neighborhood coffee shop, bar, or club; author readings and signings at a book store or library; or even a community day of service cleaning up a park or painting a school.

Now think about how social media could help you maximize those opportunities. Social media becomes a powerful way to leverage the PR benefit of your involvement as a sponsor before, during, and after the event by creating new ways for the community to gather, communicate, interact, and remember.

Before the event, use Facebook, Twitter, and YouTube to generate interest in what's coming up. Get the conversation going before the event even happens. Encourage your core team of organizers, volunteers, and beneficiaries to get online and talk about the event on your social media sites and on their own. Get them to link to each other's sites or blogs, and reTweet.

During the event, take photos and digital video (simplify the permission issue by making permission to be photographed part of the participation contract and the ticket agreement). Tweet and blog live. Have roving "reporters" with digital cameras and audio recorders gathering on-the-spot comments from participants, organizers, and attendees. Ask everyone who signs up to blog, Tweet, and invite their Facebook friends. Sign everyone up who attends as a Facebook friend and Twitter follower so you can stay in touch. Offer a prize to the person who submits the best video or digital photo collage/ slideshow and then post it on all your event social media sites (encourage everyone to re-post for more viral coverage). If you need more volunteers, ask your Twitter followers to come and help out.

After the program, get the photos, videos, and audio posted quickly. Encourage everyone who attended to write a recap of what they liked best. If you're sponsoring a sporting team, post photos, digitals, and on-the-spot blogs throughout the season, then celebrate the team's wins and accomplishments and be sure to feature profiles of the players, coaches, and volunteers. If it was a charity effort, snap photos of volunteers doing the work and share a story by the coordinator or recipient about what the project meant to those who benefited. Scholarships and pageants can feature photos of all the contestants, winning essays, videos of speeches or performances, and a profile of the winner. Of course, everything somehow mentions you, the sponsoring organization.

Make the most of local PR by contacting the reporters for your newspaper, radio, and TV outlets, and encourage them to cover the event in their social media as well as in their regular column or show. If they attend the event, get plenty of photos and put them on your social media sites. Use your tags and keywords for great searchability, and be sure to do your social bookmarking. You might even seek out local dignitaries like the mayor or council members for photos, audio, or video. Politicians will rarely decline free PR!

You can extend the benefits (for your own publicity and for the community) all year long by using social media to create an ongoing discussion about the underlying needs met by the program. So a local educational presentation on recycling or preventing diabetes could become an ongoing blog, discussion, and Facebook fan page on how concerned citizens are making a difference in the community and how others can get involved.

Social Media Spreads the Word

You can also leverage the local power of social media by rallying neighbors to help. Local animal shelters have used Twitter and Facebook to feature pets that are available for adoption, ask for volunteers, and solicit donations of fund or money when money is tight.

Most people have no idea of the variety of things that go on in their community every day. Few Americans read a daily newspaper, and many formerly local news stations now only run nationally syndicated programming. When you become the conduit to connect busy people to their community, you gain stature as a leader and visibility for your business.

For example, you could use social media to encourage local businesspeople to buy within their community to strengthen the neighborhood economy. You could also encourage consumers to shop closer to home to save gas and support local and independent businesses. Easy ways to do this while building your own brand include writing blogs about what's available locally in your area, the benefits of doing business locally, and mentioning great examples as part of your conversation.

By featuring local events, local people, and local businesses in your social media conversation, you will create a "voice" that can resonate within your community and that raises your profile in a positive way. Put your social media sites on your business card, and invite everyone you meet to friend or follow you.

At the same time that you're cultivating your neighborhood audience, don't automatically close the door to growing regional or national clientele. You'll need to create a separate social media campaign to offer your products and services outside of your community, because local happenings won't usually be a draw for long-distance clients. On the other hand, if you live in an area that is a tourist resort, a college town, or a city or region that has seen an exodus of residents due to economic circumstances, you may find that, for those who have left, there's no place like home.

For example, a favorite sports bar in a college town could retain connections with alumni who leave the area through social media. Restaurants have found gold in shipping favorite comfort foods, sauces, and dips to regular diners who moved away, and a Facebook or Twitter site can allow your expatriate audience to get a taste of home. If you operate a store, entertainment venue, or business that sees repeat business from vacationing clients, use your social media to stay in touch all year long, keeping them updated on what's new, and finding out what they'd like to see when they return to your business.

Using social media for local businesses pays off in many ways. It can build business and strengthen community ties, which wins loyal clients. By staying in touch with event participants and "alumni" who periodically return, you can improve the odds of repeat sales. And by extending your reach to clients beyond your area, you also buffer your cash flow from the ups and downs of the local economy.

Results Reminder

Never underestimate the power of providing a taste of home.

The Rule of 30

What are 30 local touch points your business has or could cultivate in the community that could be strengthened and highlighted through social media?

30

Exercises

1. Identify the community outreach activities you're already doing, and think about how to extend and promote them with social media.

2. Look for "alumni" among those who have moved out of the area but retain strong ties to family, schools, or recreation. Don't forget to include repeat vacationers or seasonal residents.

3. Play up the local angle, but don't rule out ways you could offer your product or service to a broader market by changing your packaging or distribution.

Social Media for Nonprofits

21

As social media has moved into the mainstream and attracted adult users, nonprofits have begun to take notice. Social media is appealing to nonprofits because it's a free, easy-to-use platform that can be updated without fuss or the efforts of an expensive Web designer. Even more importantly, nonprofits have discovered that their volunteers, target user audience, and even donors are already active on social media.

Start With the Outreach Goal

Nonprofits may not have exactly the same kind of business plan as a small company or a solo professional, but well-run organizations have a clear idea of their mission and their target audience. Because there are many different kinds of nonprofits, those two elements can differ widely. Here are some examples:

- A dog rescue organization specializes in rescuing breed-specific dogs and finding new homes. It

~ needs nearby volunteers to help care for the dogs, donors to pay for expenses, and families willing to adopt a pet.

~ A major medical center wants to increase its visibility to adults 40–60 years old, knowing that they are most likely to be making decisions for their own care and for the care of an aging parent.

~ An educational scholarship program wants to encourage donors and to attract students who need money for college.

~ A local food bank wants to let donors know what food items are desperately needed, and communicate last-minute staffing needs to volunteers.

~ A national nature organization wants an interactive way to educate a broader audience about endangered wildlife, alert volunteers and donors to special needs, and get feedback from the public.

These are just a few ways nonprofit organizations might use social media. There is no one right way for a nonprofit to utilize social media. What counts is that your social media strategy reinforces your top mission goal and reaches the target audience(s) associated with that goal.

Social media can help nonprofits in three key ways: 1) tell a story; 2) raise awareness and donations; and 3) interact with donors, volunteers, and the larger community.

Tell a Story

It's easier to reach a large number of people if you go where they've already congregated. Setting up a Twitter or Facebook page, blog, or YouTube or Flickr account makes it possible for your organization to share an interactive, multimedia story with hundreds of millions of people who are already congregating on social media sites.

In the past, nonprofits were limited to using an annual report to share their triumphs and challenges. Then Websites added multimedia and a global reach. But one of the limitations of both annual reports and Websites is that they require the reader to go looking for them in order to get the story.

With social media, it's possible for you to take your story to the crowd. A Facebook page not only enables you to provide frequent updates on upcoming events, volunteer opportunities, and ongoing programs, but it makes it easy to share photos and video, and to have participants post their comments and feedback. Where a Website or an annual report is a one-way monologue, social media creates a two-way dialogue. The opportunity for feedback and input can also be an important step to healing for organizations that have experienced problems that lead to decreased trust and donations.

Even more importantly, social media can be a great place to tell the story of your clients and to post case studies. Facebook and other sites make it easy to share a PowerPoint slide show or a short video highlighting success stories. These can be stories of how your organization has created successful change in the community, or case studies about how you've implemented organizational changes to save money, improve efficiency, or extend outreach. The topics for the case study can vary by the audience of each specific social media site.

For example, stories that highlight client outcomes and cost-effective outreach are most powerful on social media sites targeting the public. But you could also use LinkedIn to share non-proprietary case studies with colleagues and professional associates to highlight best practices or extend the dialogue after a conference.

Social media can also be a great place to invite volunteers, donors, and recipients of your services to share their comments and testimonials. Questions asked in the comment sections of blogs and Facebook pages give you a public forum to clear up misunderstandings or educate about the need and scope of services. Most importantly, a vibrant social media site shows your organization is engaged, open for conversation, and utilizing cost-efficient tools to share its message.

Awareness and Donations

When the massive earthquake hit Haiti in 2010, social media sites lit up with information about the situation. Relief efforts used Twitter and text messaging to mobilize volunteers and collect donations. Survivors in Haiti used social media to post photos, ask for aid, and share stories and video from the scene.

Social media played an important role in covering the Haiti earthquake because it provided a real-time opportunity to see what was happening and to hear the story in the words of those who were living through the disaster and its aftermath without any media gatekeepers. Social media also played an important role in fundraising, either by sending readers to the Websites of organizations responding to the disaster, or by collecting money through applications like the Causes widget on Facebook.

Since the success of the Obama presidential campaign, the fundraising community has realized the role social media can play in mobilizing donors and collecting a large number of small donations to make a big difference. Social media specializes in massive reach. While most traditional fundraising campaigns focus on acquiring large donations from a few wealthy donors, social media makes it possible to mobilize large numbers of small dollar donors without the cost and lengthy preparation of an annual campaign. This can be especially useful when there is a sudden, urgent need, even if it isn't a disaster on the scale of the Haiti earthquake. Imagine a local food bank with a Twitter list of dedicated local volunteers, community leaders, and corporate donors being able to alert readers to a sudden spike in traffic (requiring more volunteers on short notice) or shortages of key staple items.

Raising awareness often focuses on reaching out to new contacts, but it's important to remember that there is a very real benefit in increasing day-to-day awareness of programs and needs among your current base of donors, volunteers, sponsors and clients. In fundraising as in sales, it's generally believed that 80 percent of donations come from 20 percent of donors, and that it's easier (and less expensive) to encourage repeat donations from people who already give to your cause than to prospect for new donors. Through social media, you can stay visible to those current donors and volunteers all year long for free. Unlike with direct mail, you can share photos and video immediately after an event, or provide updates of on-the-scene response efforts. By staying visible to people who already care about your cause and who have demonstrated their willingness to donate or volunteer, you increase your chances of repeat donations and volunteer retention.

Interact With the Community

Social media makes it possible to grow your interested community without incurring extra costs. The Nonprofits on Facebook page boasts over 30,000 nonprofits using Facebook to connect with others through that social media site alone. Twellow shows more than 12,000 nonprofits listed in its directory, plus thousands of other organizations under different categories. Using the strategic friending and following tactics provided earlier in the book, you can create groups on Facebook, LinkedIn, and YouTube, or set up your own Twibe on Twitter. You can reach out to people who are already fans of similar organizations and invite them to check out your pages. And by including your social media contact buttons from AddThis. com on all your press releases and online sites, you make it easy for dedicated supporters to spread the word.

For example, the Mayo Clinic is bringing its reputation for clinical excellence to a whole new generation by repurposing interviews and videos and posting them on YouTube and Facebook. The National Wildlife Federation has multiple Twitter accounts, one for each of its major programs, to stay engaged with members and spread the word. Palomar Pomorodo West hospital in California took visitors on a virtual tour of its new facility in Second Life, generating a flurry of news coverage through both traditional news channels and social media.

Animal shelters and rescue programs like the MidAtlantic Great Dane Rescue League use Twitter and Facebook to post the appealing photos of animals in need of permanent or foster families, and to communicate with existing donors and the public about opportunities to volunteer or make cash/in-kind donations. School support organizations like Cradles to Crayons uses Twitter to let donors know which school supplies are needed by specific participating schools and tells donors where to drop off donations.

Whether your organization is local or global, and whether the need you serve is around the world or across town, social media can be a powerful way to deepen relationships with the people in your community who are most interested in your mission.

Provide a Lasting Record

People like to give to organizations that make a real difference. Social media makes it possible to engage readers and show tangible benefits by sharing a lasting record of photos, audio clips, videos, and testimonials.

Nonprofits have often used community events and education to share their message. They've also relied on being part of local gatherings, with activities that range from setting up display tables at malls or fairs to encouraging employees to participate in business networking events. All of those outreach efforts remain important. Social media can become one more tool in your community outreach arsenal, with the added benefit that, with social media, your "display" is available around the clock, 365 days a year.

Results Reminder

Social media creates one more of the 30 touches to move onlookers to action.

The Rule of 30

What are 30 tips, facts, or statistics you'd like to share with a broader audience to encourage participation?

30

Exercises

1. Determine whether you want to create an umbrella social media presence for the whole organization, or a page for each of your major programs. Let content and target audience influence your choice.

2. Your strategy should include a method to friend/ follow your existing donors and volunteers, and to selectively reach out to new people who have shown an interest in your type of program.

3. Tie your content into topics that already have the public interest, such as headlines, holidays, and awareness months. Be sure to include your own calendar of upcoming special events, fundraising campaigns, and community service days.

22 Social Media and Branding

Whether or not you've consciously created one, you have a brand. Not too long ago, most people thought "branding" was something only the largest consumer products companies and car manufacturers needed to worry about. In today's market, it's not a stretch to say that every individual in the marketplace, whether company owner, solo professional employee, or contractor needs a "brand" to stand apart from the competition.

At the heart of branding is the essence of what makes you or your company unique. This should be familiar territory for you if you've done the exercises in the first seven chapters of this book. Let's revisit some of those concepts now that you have a clearer idea of the power of social media to understand how you can use social media tools to reinforce your branding.

It Starts With a Goal and an Audience

This is a good time to pull out the matrix you created for your top business goal and target audience. The branding you create for your company, yourself, and your products/services must be aligned with your key business goals. Otherwise, the messages will be out of sync, and customers will sense that something isn't quite right. They may not recognize it as inconsistent branding, but it will be enough to send them elsewhere for solutions.

Think about the problem/pain/fear faced by the customers you most want to serve, and what it takes to get them past the ego/money obstacle. What messages are you using to build a dialogue and a relationship with this customer base? Think about all the marketing vehicles (including social media) you are currently using: advertising, direct mail, newsletters, online marketing, etc. Can you summarize the benefit/solution to the pain/problem/fear in one sentence from each of your messages? Do any of your messages address the ego/money obstacle? If so, is there a consistent thread that links the messages together?

If you have a tagline or slogan, print it out and place it next to your matrix.

Does it reinforce the impression of your company that you want to give to your best prospects? For example, if you want to reach out to a regional or national market, but your slogan says "Your Hometown Resource...," your message is mismatched to your goal. How does your tagline/slogan reinforce or contradict your branding? What about the 30-second elevator speech your give at live events or as your social media introduction? Customers will sense when the pieces of your marketing don't present a consistent and coherent image.

Values, Voice, and Story

Do you remember your Transformational Value? That's what you offer to solve the pain/problem/fear. It offers to transform your customers by helping them achieve their top business goal or overcome their biggest obstacle. A statement of your Transformational Value should be woven into your messages, on social media and in your other advertising as well. Your best prospects have a number of competing options to solve their problem. The social media messages you craft should always have a clear reminder of how you help your customers transform themselves beyond their current limitations.

In the early chapters of the book, I showed you how to find the Real Story of your business—the wellspring of passion that drove you to create your company or professional practice. Your Real Story is another way in which you and your business are unique. No one else has followed the same journey or is moved by exactly the same passion as you. That journey and passion will resonate with the readers you are meant to best serve. Your Real Story becomes part of your Transformational Value because you bring a perspective honed by your journey and passion that alters the way you provide your services. Social media is a great format to tell and retell your Real Story with text, photos, audio, and video.

Your True Voice is the collection of words and phrases that most naturally describe your services and the benefit they provide. True Voice words are honest and compelling, and they feel right when you use them to talk about your company. Nothing about your True Voice feels forced, phony, or contrived. You are speaking from the heart, and that resonates with your listeners and readers on a subconscious level. Your True Voice, when aligned with your top business goals, best audience, Real Story, and Transformational Value, becomes enormously charismatic. Because you're speaking from passion and a mission to solve the problem/pain/fear, your True Voice has power. Social media enables you to share your True Voice through the words you choose for your blog posts, Tweets, and online articles, as well as the way in which you share your news with friends on Facebook, LinkedIn, and other sites. Your True Voice can come through in your Web audio and video.

Your Irresistible Difference is the "something extra" you provide that your competitors don't. It's the way you exceed expectations by offering not just what your customers *say* they want, but what they really need and didn't put into words, and what they're hoping to find and are afraid to ask. The Irresistible Difference goes beyond satisfying customers to delighting them by providing what they didn't think they could ever find. For example, if you provide repair services, your customer might be resigned to wait all day for a service call, wasting time and growing frustrated. Provide an Irresistible Difference of a repair person who shows up at a fixed appointment time, and it will delight customers for whom time is money.

Avoiding a Case of Mistaken Identity

If your logo is badly designed, looks outdated, or doesn't translate well to the Web, your prospects will pick up subtle clues that you don't really have your act together. If you're not using your logo on your social media sites, or if the design elements of your blog header, Twitter background, and other sites don't look like they belong together, your customer will get a subconscious negative feeling that "something doesn't add up." That disconnect affects how the prospect perceives your professionalism, and it makes the customer wonder whether you're who you claim to be. That doubt will cost you business.

"Graphic identity" is the term for the colors, font styles, logo elements, and visual presentation of your company. For best results, your graphic identity should be the same whether a prospect picks up a brochure, reads a business card, or connects to your blog or Facebook page. Graphic identity provides a subconscious reassurance that your story checks out, which helps the prospect see you as truthful and consistent.

Open up your Website, Facebook, LinkedIn, Twitter, and blog in separate browser windows on your screen so you can see them all at the same time. If you have other social media profiles, open them as well. Now try to view your online presence the way a new prospect would see you. Look across all your social media sites and answer these questions:

~ Are the photos the same for all your profiles? Do you look friendly and smiling? Are you dressed professionally with good grooming?

~ Are you using colors from your logo consistently? Do you retain the same color palette from site to site?

~ Does your logo look good online? (If it's pixilated, stretched, or blurry, a graphic designer can produce your logo in a sharp Web resolution at minimal cost.)

~ Do you use consistent type fonts that are appealing to your best target audience (think age, media exposure, and eyesight)?

~ Do the graphic elements as a group convey the right "feel" for your brand? As a whole, do your sites look modern, professional, trendy, conservative, or edgy? Is that the impression you want to give?

~ If you're using photos and video, are you unconsciously excluding some of your best prospects by not including them in your visuals? Unless you serve a niche audience defined by gender, age, or ethnicity, your photos should have an inclusive, diverse mix of people to provide the unspoken clue that you welcome diverse customers.

Your brand is a combination of Transformational Value, Real Story, True Voice, Irresistible Difference and graphic identity, that creates a unique, compelling, and memorable personality woven through everything you do. When you're consistent in carrying your branding throughout your social media, the authenticity and credibility will resonate with your best prospects to help motivate them toward action.

Results Reminder

Every online marketing touch reinforces or detracts from your brand.

The Rule of 30

What are 30 ways in which you can use branding elements to strengthen the consistency and cohesiveness of your social media messages?

30

Exercises

1. Write down your Transformational Value, Real Story, True Voice, Irresistible Difference, and graphic identity, then create consistency across your social media sites.

2. Ask a group of prospects to be a focus group and have them give you their impressions. Compare the test group's impressions to the identity you want to convey with your brand, and make the changes to bring brand and perception into alignment.

Going Global With Social Media

23

First, let me challenge the idea of a "local" business in the age of Internet commerce and knowledge-based economy. Every company in the world began as a local business. If you think there are reasons why your company is intrinsically local, I want you to reexamine those factors.

Is it because your business model has relied on face-to-face service? Do you provide a perishable product, such as food? Is your service fundamentally hands-on, such as massage, home and office organization, or dog training? Are there licensing restrictions or laws governing the provision of your service, such as those in law or medicine?

I want you to brainstorm which elements of your current product or service could be repackaged to reach a broader audience. If you run a restaurant, you might not be able to mail your barbecue ribs across the country, but you could bottle and ship the sauce. You can't ship a hot cup of coffee, but you can sell the beans, flavorings, and logo mugs through e-commerce.

Licensing restrictions may dictate where you can physically practice law or medicine, but a book on your subject can reach readers around the world. Massage, fitness, organization, and other hands-on specialties can go far beyond a local audience through video and how-to books.

Low-cost global phone service also makes it easier than ever before to offer coaching or consulting via phone calls, teleseminars, or even group-coaching Webinars. Take a few moments and think about how you might be able to package your products and services to reach the world.

Make sure you haven't prematurely closed off options for growth by thinking too small. Can your company "productize" what it offers to reach a larger audience? You might be able to increase your sales both at home and abroad with an expanded and easily shipped product line. Reaching a broader audience also helps to "recession-proof" your business, because even difficult economic times rarely hit all areas equally. By working with a national or global audience, you stand a better chance of bringing in a steady flow of new business even if your local area is experiencing a slow period.

The Global Company Next Door

It used to be that global sourcing was something only the largest companies could consider. Now, anyone with an Internet connection can shop for the best deal from online stores all over the world. Amazon, eBay, and other online retailers have made it unimportant where an item is physically stored, and they enable buyers to compare prices and purchase items almost without geographic constraints.

Did you realize that Amazon, eBay, and the online staffing site Elance.com are also special types of social media? Authors who have books available on Amazon can create Amazon author pages. These pages give authors the ability to post a blog and will automatically update everyone who has purchased that author's books through Amazon whenever a new post is made.

eBay may be one of the worlds' largest shopping sites, but for companies that offer their wares through the site, eBay is also a vibrant social media community with blogs, user forums, and lots of behind-the-scenes interactions among the retailers—large and small—who sell on this giant site.

Elance.com is an online staffing site that enables companies to hire a wide variety of talented professionals for one-time or ongoing projects. It also makes it possible for small companies and solo professionals to offer their talents for sale to a global marketplace from the comfort of their home or office. Elance makes it possible for companies to post projects, invite specific providers to bid, view online portfolios, and interact via private chat and forum boards with providers who could be in the next state or on the other side of the world. Elance also has its own blog and chat rooms for providers to learn strategies to better utilize the site and interact with each other and Elance administrators. Providers let employers know about themselves by posting social media–style profile pages that they can embellish with testimonials, photos, and portfolios.

The point is that customers have become accustomed to buying products and services without face-to-face interaction. Buyers have also learned to shop for pricing, features, and qualifications online. At the same time, companies have grown more confident in telecommuting, whether their employees are working from home or based in another country. Companies have also become more savvy about recognizing that talent does not have an even geographic distribution, and that specially qualified individuals can make a valuable contribution without physically coming into the office.

Social Media Makes the Connection

Social media sites such as Facebook and Twitter offer another opportunity to meet prospective clients from all over the world. By utilizing their networking capabilities to engage prospects in conversation before focusing on making a sale, you have the opportunity to tap into markets that would have been geographically prohibitive.

Alumni, club, and association sites also present opportunities for global networking. Most colleges and universities retain ties with alumni who are working or living out of the country. These expatriates might be receptive to working with someone who shares familiar ties and perspectives. Clubs and associations with international memberships offer the chance for you to get to know fellow members around the world with the immediate connection of a shared affiliation. Online profiles and membership directories, plus forum or chat areas within the club/association Website, make connecting easy.

LinkedIn is a great way to reclaim connections with colleagues who are now living abroad. You can also leverage the connections of your own network of colleagues to ask for introductions to their foreign colleagues or to the overseas branch of their organization. It's never been easier to see the web of personal connections, and that network makes the world a very small neighborhood.

Social media also makes it easy to share your information without geographic boundaries. By sharing tips, uploading case studies, or providing links to videos on your Facebook or Twitter sites, you are reaching a worldwide audience of prospects with a built-in mechanism for two-way interaction. Always review your content for unintentional language that might limit your perceived willingness to work with companies or individuals outside of the country. For example, unless the content is specific to the laws or conditions of a particular place, use more inclusive words such as *customers* instead of nationality-limited words such as *American* or *Canadian*. You can also make it clear on your Website and in your profile and social media bio that you work with clients worldwide, or at least beyond your own national borders.

If you're already selling products worldwide, make a conscious effort to include the customers you might never meet face to face through your social media strategy. For example, my fiction books sell to an international readership. I can't visit everyone's local bookstore, but I wanted to make more personal connections. So in addition to my social media outreach, I've created two annual, online, blog-tour events and make an effort to invite bloggers and Websites based around the world to participate. Making the effort to be inclusive definitely gets noticed.

If you're interested in reaching a particular part of the world, be sure to look at which social media sites are most popular in those countries. The list of sites and their popularity changes constantly, but doing a Google search on "social media in Europe" or "social media in South America" should give you a good idea of which sites are local favorites. Remember that not all sites use English as their primary language, so if you're bilingual you may be able to participate in a broader variety of non-English sites.

Social media is a great way to expand your company's horizons. By productizing your existing services, participating in global marketplaces like eBay or Elance, or adding new services such as teleclasses, phone coaching, or online group coaching, you can serve a broader audience and satisfy a global need for the expertise you provide.

Results Reminder

Challenge your assumed geographic boundaries. The world awaits you!

The Rule of 30

Look for 30 people or identify 30 opportunities to connect to prospects, colleagues, or partners to begin your international outreach.

30

Exercises

1. Use the free Google Analytics service to see what countries are already sending users to your Website. If your product is distributed worldwide, make sure you understand the specifics of where you are most popular, then utilize that information to match up with the right social media sites.

2. As you develop products and services, think about how you could provide them in a location-independent way.

3. As part of your strategic social media outreach, make an effort to connect with new friends and followers from areas outside the country where you'd like to see sales increase.

Social Media and Your Website

24

What does the world see when it comes to your Website? After all, most social media sites allow you to list one or more home pages or blogs. It's not uncommon for someone who meets you on Facebook or Twitter to hop over to your Website to learn more. You probably do the same thing when you're thinking of asking a contact you met on social media to provide a product or service.

Many Websites sprawl like an untended garden. Few people have a clear idea of what they want from their Web presence before they put up a site (or, at least, their first site). Some site owners just add pages for new material, but pay little attention to update or remove old information. Other sites are essentially abandoned, having been posted and then ignored.

Your Website is your virtual storefront and business card. Rightly or wrongly, people will judge you by the quality and content of your site. This is especially true if the information they see on social media about you doesn't seem to match the Website when they visit. When a social media friend makes the effort to check out your Website, you're one step closer to closing a sale. Don't let them slip out the front door.

Back to Basics

In the beginning of this book, you learned how to prioritize your business goals, identify the key target audience to achieve those goals, and hone in on the message that will move your audience from prospect to customer. But you might be surprised to find out how few people seem to remember those guidelines when they create a Website. The principles that apply to your social media also apply to your Website.

Take a hard look at your existing site. Is it outdated? Are your photo and bio current? Does it showcase your most recent accomplishments and accolades? Do you have badges for Facebook, Twitter, and LinkedIn to help your Web visitors meet you on social media?

A great way to get twice the impact out of your writing time is to have your blog and your Twitter page feed content (via RSS) to the homepage of your Website. That way, every time you post a new blog or Tweet, your homepage gets updated content. Your homepage always looks fresh, and search engines will pick up your site because it's frequently updated. It's a winning solution!

You can also embed YouTube videos or Flickr photos into your Website. This is another great way to get more productivity out of your social media time by making each element work for you in multiple places. The YouTube videos you create with your digital video recorder won't look studio quality, but that's okay. If your content is good and the short videos are lively and packed with personality, viewers will have the feeling that they've met you, which is a great way to take the online relationship one step forward.

Audio is another way to personalize your site and let visitors get to know you. AudioAcrobat.com is one of my favorite tools because it's easy to use and versatile. You can record a personal Web audio so that you greet every visitor to the site, and then easily add the audio to your homepage. Consider having a different personal audio greeting for every page. (You can add a link to the audio on your Facebook page and in your Twitter bio as well!)

If you've always wanted to be on the radio, consider doing a podcast. A podcast is a lot like a radio show, except that it is recorded, not live, and is broadcast via the Internet. Podcasts can be anywhere from five minutes to two hours in length. (I'd suggest 15 minutes or less.) You can record a daily tip or insight, or interview guests. Podcasts can also be fed to your Website via RSS (and to your other social media sites as well), creating yet another interesting element, and an additional way for prospects to get to know you. It doesn't require a lot of equipment or technical knowledge to podcast (you can start with a phone and AudioAcrobat), but it can be a great cross-promotional tool, as well as a way to connect with a broader audience and share your expertise.

Your Homepage Portal

With social media, your homepage actually becomes a portal, a gateway Website that lets viewers start at a central location and then easily find a wide variety of information. From your homepage, in addition to the standard Web information such as an About Us page, a page of products or services, and perhaps an online purchase page, you can feed your main blog, Tweets, and even a podcast into your site to keep it relevant and fresh.

There's no law that restricts you to just one blog. One of the main reasons many business owners have outdated Web content is because of the cost of having their designer update the pages. Take another look at your site and determine which pages may only need a once-a-year freshening, and which pages should be updated weekly or monthly. Frequently updated pages can be fed by creating new, special-purpose blogs that make it easy and inexpensive for you (or a virtual assistant) to update regularly.

For example, you could create a blog that is just for your speaking engagements, open houses, book signings, or educational programs and have it feed the Upcoming Events page on your Website. Your content will be in two places at once (the blog and your site), doubling your exposure to readers and search engines, and you will be able to make changes quickly and inexpensively.

I believe every site should have a News page to highlight your announcements, new clients, awards, appearances, and other newsworthy activities. This can be another page that lends itself to a blog feed. Create another special-purpose blog just for press releases, links to recent articles that feature your company, audio links to radio or podcast interviews, and photos from your business travel or events. If you post articles online in article directories such as eZineArticles.com, be sure to include the link to your expert page or links to individual articles. Once the blog feed is set up, it's easy for your virtual assistant to add new releases every month.

If you sell your products online, you may want to use a redirect page to send buyers to your eBay page or whatever online shopping cart you use. Again, this reduces redundant work, because you don't want to have to list, price, and manage all your products on multiple carts. (Remember that your shopping-cart site also functions as its own social media site with forums, blogs, and chats for members.) If you accept online bids to provide services, link to your Elance.com, Guru.com, or other marketplace site to take advantage of the structure they've built and centralize your job sourcing.

Make the Most of Social Bookmarking and Boilerplates

When you use social bookmarking to draw attention to an article, blog post, or news release, or when you create the boilerplate company information at the end of a press release, remember that you can use a link to pages beyond your home page. Search engines actually reward you for doing this, as it drives traffic deeper into the site, encouraging readers to stay and decreasing your "bounce rate." Customers like links to specific pages that feature the item mentioned in the article or release, because it saves them the time of hunting around on your site to find it.

The same principle works for your Web address on social media sites. Defaulting to your homepage may not always be the best link if there is another page more focused to the interests of that particular target audience. For example, if you're an author and you use social media sites targeted to publishers and other writers, consider using a Web address for a page on your site that talks about your books. A speaker might want to encourage readers to visit the event booking page.

Your e-mail or blog-post signature block can also change depending on the audience. When you comment in blogs, groups, and forums, consider using a link to the page on your site best suited to the topic. Readers have very little patience for rummaging through a Website looking for relevant copy. Keep them engaged by taking them right to the good stuff.

Results Reminder

Time is precious. Use your 30 minutes a day wisely by making everything you do serve more than one purpose.

The Rule of 30

Can you find 30 ways to connect your Website and your social media so that they reinforce each other, leverage your effort, and provide the most content benefit?

30

Exercises

1. Rethink your Website with your top business goal, top target audience, and new social media in mind. Where are the opportunities to reinforce your message?

2. What path through your Website would you want visitors from each of your social media sites to take? What will meet there needs or provide some of those seven to 30 touches? Once you've designed the path page by page, set up your referring links to lead visitors down the best path for their interests.

Great Sites Beyond the Ordinary

25

For some business owners and professionals, just keeping an updated presence on a few social media sites is a daunting task, even allotting 30 minutes a day to the process. But others thrive on connecting, and if you can juggle a few more sites without burning out, use your 30 minutes to explore some specialized sites worth a second look.

Wikipedia

Wikipedia is based on the premise that if everyone pools knowledge, the right answers will surface eventually. It's an online encyclopedia where everyone can contribute, edit, correct, and update information. Though it's not perfect, it's often a first stop for searchers looking for information on an unfamiliar category, making it a very high-traffic site.

Although Wikipedia frowns on any kind of promotional material, there are ways to get yourself and your company onto Wikipedia legitimately. For example, if you've patented a product or created a proprietary process, post a Wikipedia page about the product or process, citing yourself or your company as the creator. Authors, speakers, and business owners whose companies have achieved prominence are also legitimate candidates for a Wikipedia profile. Wikipedia isn't a directory of companies, so there needs to be a valid reason for your inclusion.

On sites like Wikipedia that rely on member contribution of time and content, approximately 90 percent of the information is provided and edited by about 10 percent of the users. You can connect with that active core via Wikipedia's member at its internal communications areas, the Village Pump and Community Portal.

WikiHow

A "wiki" is a user-generated knowledge base. WikiHow is a user-written article bank. This site lets you write and upload how-to articles to share your expertise. You'll get credit as the article "originator," but remember that anyone can edit and add to the information. This site is very content-focused, so outright promotion is not permitted.

SmallBusinessBrief.com

This entrepreneur-focused online community allows members to upload articles while increasing the writer's visibility and sending traffic to their site. SmallBusinessBrief.com offers a list of short article abstracts, and when readers click through, they're taken to a page on the author's home Website, which can feature the authoring company's logo and the author's photo. It's a nice news digest for a targeted audience, and regular participation could result in enhanced credibility with its regular readers.

Care2.com

A great site for green companies, health-related companies, and lifestyle/wellness coaches, Care2.com is dedicated to living a healthier life on a healthier planet. Members can upload articles and connect with each other on blogs and in topic-specific groups.

Newsvine.com

For everyone who ever wanted to be a syndicated columnist, this site is for you. Newsvine members can write their own regular columns, and post them to entertain and inform site members and regular readers. Like the social bookmarking sites, Newsvine also lets you flag articles published elsewhere that you thought would be of interest to others, and read the recommended links to articles selected by the site membership. It's an eclectic bunch, but it's one more site that subscribes to the idea that the "wisdom of crowds" just might be onto something.

Yahoo Answers and Yahoo Groups

Yahoo Answers is a site where you can build online visibility and become the go-to expert for advice or information on specific topics. There's a broad range of business and lifestyle topics, and an even wider spectrum of opinions and experience, but consistently good information tends to rise like cream.

Yahoo Groups is a way to build your own online community by creating a group around a specific topic, industry, or interest. You can also join an existing group and get to know the members, post and answer questions, and join the conversation. Like most online communities, Yahoo Groups frowns on spammers, pitchmen, and people who don't want to enter into the spirit of the group.

Moodle

Moodle itself isn't a social networking site, but its online classroom software could help you build your own destination. If you've ever taken an online group-coaching course that had an Internet-based shared classroom, you've seen Moodle or one of its competitors. Moodle lets you build a shared space where participants can work together on documents, communicate via private forum, upload their student profiles, receive assignments from the instructor, and upload homework. Although a full Moodle installation is large for most coaches or online instructors' needs, their Support page lists a number of partners that create as-needed classrooms.

Ning.com

A site for people who want to create their own social networks, Ning.com uses a template to get you up and running quickly. Members can post profiles of themselves, ask and answer questions in a forum, and create their own internal blogs. The site supports RSS (inward and outward) so users can post their Ning blog elsewhere or import a feed from outside of Ning. Ning communities are private and invitation-only, so they can be an easy way to create a user group or client-only site with lots of interactive features, without the expense of building out a custom site.

GetSatisfaction.com

GetSatisfaction isn't a social media site in itself, but it provides an inexpensive solution for companies that want to create an online support desk without paying for a custom solution. In effect, you're creating a highly targeted social media network for your users and support personnel where the emphasis is on asking questions and getting answers rather than meeting new people.

Social Media for Cell Phones

Cell phone applications to connect with social media sites are launched or updated almost daily. But if you use a cell phone with WiFi capability and especially if you use a BlackBerry, iPhone, or Droid, check for applications that allow you to monitor and update your favorite social media sites from anywhere.

Why would you want to do this? It depends. Tweeting or posting comments, photos, and video from a live event gives your readers a unique perspective on a conference or trade show. Apps that allow you to access programs like PayPal or eBay give you the ability to transact business wherever you are. Blogging when a great idea hits you could make it easier to post more frequently or comment on breaking news. You probably won't post a full article, but you might dash off a timely insight.

Applications are available to update and monitor Facebook, Twitter, YouTube, and other sites via cell phone. There are instant messaging and photo upload apps you can use from your phone.

Foursquare is a combination game and social media site where users can check in from businesses or leisure locations and earn points, gain rewards, and find out what their friends are doing. For businesses like bars, coffee houses, theaters, performance venues, and tourist or nightlife locales, Foursquare can be a new customer appreciation tool. Google's Buzz integrates the ability to monitor and upload to social media on the go. As the use of smart mobile phones grows, expect to see more ways to manage your social media empire from anywhere via your phone.

Results Reminder

Get more from your 30 minutes a day by being in the right social media sites with applications that make you more productive.

The Rule of 30

Take 30 minutes and check out a few specialized social media sites as well as the applications that come with your mobile phone.

30

Exercises

1. Be honest with yourself about how much time and energy you want to invest in social media. Remember that the investment should be linked to accomplishing your top business goal. Don't spread yourself too thin.

2. Develop a measurement that is meaningful to you so you can gauge return on investment (ROI) for your time. Will you be satisfied with an increase in Web traffic, a large number of friends or fans, expert status on forum boards, or solid leads for new business?

3. Start with one to three core sites and spend the time to really get to know the community and contribute before adding additional sites. Use a virtual assistant to post news, but make sure you're the one actually answering questions and connecting with friends/fans.

26 Social Media and Events

Successful events require a lot of time and energy. This is true whether the event is live or virtual. Social media can help you create more interesting events, attract a wide audience, and preserve an event so that it continues to provide benefit long after the tables and booths are put away.

Building an Audience

One reason for maintaining a presence in social media is to create a relationship with people who are interested in what you offer and what you have to say. So when you're planning an event, make sure you talk the event up to your social media friends and followers, and give them a VIP invitation. Go beyond just an announcement of the event date and title. You can use your blog, Twitter, and other social media sites to talk about the behind-the-scenes effort and insights that go into building an event. Tell them about your hopes for the event and what value you want to create for your audience. Make them feel like they're part of the team before the doors ever open. You may even want to create a special early-bird pricing that you promote only to your dedicated social media fans and followers as a reward.

As you build out the event, blog and Tweet about the guests, vendors, and entertainers. Talk up the food and networking. Use Facebook to share photos of speakers with their bios. Introduce your event team and the roles they play. Whet readers' appetites for what you're creating and make it tangible with a high perceived value. You could even shoot some digital video of the event setup, and catch vendors and speakers talking casually about what they're looking forward to in the event and what value they offer to attendees. In today's reality show culture, getting a look at the "drama" behind the show is almost expected. You could go a step further and script your own "reality" show video to encourage attendance.

As you promote your event, don't overlook Meetup.com. This site is location-specific by city and zip code, and it's a great way to begin to build an audience long before your big event. Anyone can start a Meetup group. Groups are sorted by topic, so newcomers can easily find groups they want to join according to their interest. You can use your Meetup group to promote teleclasses and webinars in addition to live events, and you can build buzz for a big annual event by getting the group together for coffee or lunch. This can also be a beta group for your larger event ideas, providing an opportunity to try out workshop topics or gather input on high-interest subjects.

Don't forget to let the other groups and clubs you regularly participate in on social media know all about your big event. You can invite group members (make it a sincere invitation and not a mass-produced spammy advertisement) to attend, and comment during the development process to build awareness. You can also take advantage of the group's collective knowledge by asking for recommendations and referrals for venues, resources, entertainers, connections to speakers, and other logistical elements. Contact the leader of the live and online membership groups of which you've been an active member and ask if he/she would be willing to offer a discounted special ticket price to that organization's memberships to support a fellow member's event.

Make the Most of Live and Virtual Events

Use the power of social media to take your live promotions online and to create virtual events. By doing so, you can dramatically increase the impact and reach of events that otherwise might have been limited by weather, geography, or traffic conditions.

When you're hosting a live promotional event, think about how to provide opportunities to participate live via social media. Have someone responsible for creating short digital videos and uploading them to YouTube during the event. Tweet and blog live from the event, and post photos of contests, speakers, entertainers, and participants. Host a live chat during the event, and encourage event attendees to Tweet live via cell phone or to upload cell-phone photos or video on site for an as-it-happens feel. (Make sure to get signed video release forms from presenters for any presentations you videotape to avoid conflicts about copyright. Make the video release part of the ticketing agreement for all attendees so that anyone who attends has already given permission to show up on video.)

Augment the live event by adding online-only additional content posted through your social media sites. Give presenters the opportunity to contribute guest blogs, and encourage them to blog on their own sites before, during, and after the live event. Have a central online connection where speakers or key participants can upload Tweets or comments. Host an online chat or forum where people who couldn't attend or didn't get their questions answered during the live event can do a Q&A session with the experts. Offer presenters the chance to provide additional information or links to expanded material on your social media sites so participants can extend and deepen the experience. Make it possible for social media followers to submit questions that can be asked by an intermediary during the event, and then blog or Tweet the replies.

You can also utilize these strategies for online events, such as virtual trade shows and Webinars. Without the constraints of venue space or room rental time limits, your event can continue in social media for as long as participants are interested, and can live on virtually forever.

Contests and Awards to Build Your Buzz

Whether your event is live or virtual, consider adding some contests and award presentations to spice up the program, create more reasons for publicity, and engage pre-existing groups to participate.

For example, you could create a contest open to everyone (no purchase necessary) that shows a creative use of your product. (Heinz Ketchup did a great job encouraging users to make their own mini-videos of their favorite use of ketchup and then uploading them to the Heinz site.) Promise to screen the best entries and present the award at the event. Now you have two more reasons to send out relevant press releases: the contest itself and the winner.

Creating an award works in much the same way. You can choose someone notable in your industry, a community leader, or an author with a relevant book your topic and present an award for achievement, being a major industry influence, or leadership. Invite the winner to attend to receive the award. You can also invite the public and your friends/followers to submit names for consideration. Now you've got three reasons for press coverage: the award application process, the award winner, and the presentation at the event. Not only that, but finalists and the winner are sure to mention the award and your event to their newsletter readers and their social media friends and followers.

Recycle and Repurpose Your Events

With social media, your event doesn't have to end when it's over. Social media offers a great opportunity to recycle and repurpose your event materials and programming to extend the event's reach far beyond the initial live audience.

For example, the audio or Web video of presentations can be offered as a free or paid Webinar or download. (Make sure to arrange this with any presenters first.) If you've taped the entire event, the DVD can become a product. (Again, be sure your contract with speakers establishes who owns the rights to the DVD of the event.) You can also break a long Web video or Webinar into short, less-than-five-minute segments and do a series of YouTube videos to reach a broader audience.

Content created for presentations can be reused for blog posts and articles. Follow up on popular presentations with an additional question-and-answer session with the presenter and post it on your blog. Invite speakers to submit follow-up articles and guest blog posts. Hold spinoff workshops or seminars based on the most popular topics. Look for ways to continue to partner with your speakers and vendors so that you can both remain visible to the other's newsletter and social media audiences.

Social media can make it easy and affordable to extend the life of your online or live events, and can create opportunities to maximize your sales promotions while encouraging customer participation.

Results Reminder

Just announcing an event on social media doesn't guarantee an audience. How will you engage friends, fans, and followers in the process?

The Rule of 30

What are 30 touches you can use to promote your event before, during, and after the presentation date using social media?

30

Exercises

1. How can you engage customers in participating in your events and promotions via social media? Looking at your scheduled events, which ones lend themselves to customer-generated videos, photos, Tweets, or live blogging? Where could you capture Web audio or video testimonials? How can you reward customers who use social media to share your events and promotions?

2. Don't forget the simple stuff. Use your Facebook, Twitter, and blog to remind readers of upcoming events, encourage them to bring their digital cameras or Tweet/blog live from the event, and recognize those who participate.

27 Social Media and the Author

Authors today face a daunting challenge. Estimates for new books published annually range from 200,000 to 400,000, depending on what's included and who's counting. That's a lot of competition. Walk into any bookstore, and you'll see thousands of titles competing for the reader's attention and pocketbook. Do an Internet search and you'll find thousands more e-books, audio books, and self-published books along with the small press and traditionally published books. Many communities have seen local bookstores vanish and library hours cut for budget reasons.

Writing the book is the easy part. Promoting the book to its most likely readers is the challenge.

Social media can help authors cut through the clutter, connect with readers and influencers (such as bookstore buyers and librarians), and retain a relationship with readers and reviewers between books. Social media is also a way to add sight, sound, and motion to the larger experience around your books, and to help you jump off the page as an interesting personality worthy of media attention.

Make the Connection

One of the best ways you can get people talking about your new book is through social media. Create a fan page for your book on Facebook and a site on MySpace. Open a Twitter account under your own name, and make sure you include your publishing professional connections on LinkedIn. Use your blog and Website as a media platform under your control to talk about the book and related topics.

What else is there to talk about aside from the fact that the book has a publication date? Plenty. As you arrange signings, speaking engagements, and live appearances, you should blog, post, and Tweet about them. Look for tie-ins to recent headlines that you can address in blog posts and online articles (tying into headlines makes your article or post highly search-engine friendly). As you meet other authors, offer to swap blog posts or do guest blogging on topics related to your subject or industry (for nonfiction books) or to your genre or topic for fiction books.

Whether your book is fiction or nonfiction, use the audience connection strategies mentioned earlier in this book to find where your potential readers are already congregating. Facebook, Twitter, and MySpace have plenty of genre-specific groups for fiction writers to tap into, and topic-related groups perfect for nonfiction authors. Remember: Don't spam or do a hard sell. Make sure your book title and book Website are part of your signature block, and then begin to interact with the existing communities by answering forum questions, posting blog comments, and inviting readers who share your interests to check out your site and be your fan, friend, or follower.

Readers like to feel that they are getting to know the person behind the book. After all, that's the appeal of meeting an author at a book signing or live event. No matter how active you are in personally promoting your book, you won't be able to visit every community, so use social media to bridge the gap. Create a welcome video for your homepage. Cut a Web audio greeting, and record yourself reading the first chapter. Let your personality shine through in your blog posts and Tweets.

Compile your own list of book reviewers, librarians, and bookstore managers and send a personalized e-mail introducing yourself and your book, and looking for ways to connect. Don't forget to include book clubs, authors' groups, and local chapters of genre or professional organizations interested in your topic. Rather than including any attachments (many people won't open anything from someone they don't know, and some firewalls screen out attachments), include a link to your book Website. Offer to send a review copy, speak to the group, or mention your willingness to write an article or guest blog.

Remain on the Radar

If you're publishing multiple books, it's important to retain a connection with readers between books, because attention spans are short. A reader who loved your first book may have forgotten about it by the time the second book comes out. Use social media to stay in touch with readers and provide updates on the progress of the new book, links to reviews or interviews, new videos, or audio from radio programs on which you were featured as a guest.

You can keep the conversation fresh and inject some fun by doing extras like trivia questions, surveys, and polls. Don't forget to use social bookmarking when you get a good review, have an article published, or see your Internet radio interview posted online. You can also pass these links along to your readers on your social media sites. Friend and follow other authors as you meet them and reTweet their posts to build goodwill.

Social media makes it easy for authors who are physically separated to cross-promote each other. Most readers will read multiple books in a year, so if you can gain visibility with a similar author's readership (and offer that visibility to your own readership to them in return), you both gain. It's like having a referral by a trusted friend. Exchanging blog posts is one way authors can use social media to cross promote, as it reTweeting interesting links and comments. You can also share a blog on a permanent basis, which reduces each author's time commitment to keeping the blog fresh. You can also offer downloadable freebies from other author friends as a bonus to readers who pre-order or buy your book online, and encourage your author friends to do the same for you. Everyone loves free samples. You're limited only by your imagination.

Consider creating annual online events, especially if you are writing a series of books or have new book-related products in the pipeline. Blog tours are very popular, and can create global awareness without ever requiring you to leave home. Start by identifying a dozen or so bloggers who already reach your target audience. Find a week in your calendar to designate as your blog tour, and contact bloggers asking to do a guest blog, interview, or questions and answers during that blog-tour week. Promise to promote the event up front, during, and afterward to provide them with new visibility. You can also include free downloadable chapter samples, bonus Web audio or video, and the opportunity to answer blog comments live during a specified time.

Internet radio has shows dedicated to every fiction and nonfiction topic. These shows usually offer longer interviews than broadcast stations do, and reach a loyal niche audience. YouTube is a great way to post video blogs from your live appearances. You can also post your book-related travel or event photos via Flickr to add live and personality to your site throughout the year.

Readers Love Social Media

Social media offers a treasure trove of sites just for authors, readers, and book lovers. Here are a few to check into:

~ Shelfari.com enables readers and authors to create a virtual bookshelf of their favorite books and encourages members to recommend books. There's usually lively discussion about books as well as readers seeking suggestions of new books.

~ BookTour.com gives authors the chance to post their upcoming events, and connects readers to author readings and signings in their zip code area.

~ Bookmarket.ning.com is an online community of dedicated readers and authors who love to talk about books, publishing, and writing. It's a great place to get to know people and explore what's new.

~ Amazon.com offers authors of books posted for sale on Amazon the chance to have a free profile page and blog. Your Amazon author blog is automatically sent out to all the people who have purchased your book via Amazon, which is a great way to stay in touch with readers you wouldn't otherwise have a way to contact.

~ AuthorNation.com is another free membership site where authors, readers, and publishers connect and talk about books and writing.

~ GoodReads.com is an book lover's site. The focus is on discovering, discussing, and recommending new books. The site loves authors and is a great way to connect with readers.

~ BlogTalkRadio.com is your gateway to finding thousands of Internet radio shows and podcasts about your topic or genre. Many shows are well-established with a loyal and large audience. Most importantly, these shows speak to highly targeted niche listeners who may be the perfect audience for your book.

~ RedRoom.com is a thriving community of authors and readers covering a wide range of topics and genres.

~ Meetup.com features many writing groups and local book clubs, making it a perfect way to find groups that might want you as a guest author!

~ Podiobooks.com makes it easy for authors to record and distribute their book in an audio format. It also has an active online community of authors, listeners, and friends.

New sites spring up almost daily, and there are many sites that specialize in a particular topic or genre. Find your best fit and start connecting!

Results Reminder

The publisher cannot do enough to promote your book by itself. Use social media for effective, affordable, and targeted outreach.

The Rule of 30

How can you create 30 touches through social media to connect with readers and let the world know about your book?

30

Exercises

1. Explore the groups and Twibes dedicated to your genre or topic. Look for ways to connect to those existing audiences.

2. Think about what promotional freebies (free chapters, video, audio, etc.) you can offer via social media.

3. Make a list of 30 tips and topics related to your book that you can use as blog posts or Tweets.

28 Social Media and the Speaker

Speakers today face tough competition. Economic uncertainty has led many companies and organizations to scale back on events and to renegotiate speaker fees and reimbursement. Despite those hardships, speaking to groups is still an important income stream for many experts and a way to gain recognition for coaches, consultants, and authors.

Much of the advice for authors in the previous chapter can also be applied for speakers. Many speakers also have books or info products they've written, so they can benefit from promoting both their books and their availability as a speaker. Social media can lend a hand.

Provide a Free Sample

Event organizers are understandably reluctant to book a speaker they've never seen. You can use Web video to help overcome that reluctance by providing planners with a free sample of your speaking technique. Planners may check out your Website before contacting you for a full-demo DVD, so a couple of short clips that show your strengths as a presenter may be enough to encourage them to move further with the process of booking you for their event.

Don't stop with posting clips to your main Website. Utilize video on your Facebook and LinkedIn sites, and Tweet about new YouTube videos when you post them. You can also include your new videos on your blog, with the opportunity to add extra commentary or insights.

Event planners like to see evidence that you're in demand as a speaker. Blog and Tweet about your upcoming events, and update your Facebook and LinkedIn status when you're heading out for events, and when you post photos, video, or a recap after the event. When you speak, invite listeners to become your social media friends, fans, and followers, and encourage them to post comments on what has been most helpful about your presentation.

Work with event promoters before and after the events where you speak. Offer to provide guest blogs or articles related to your topic, and be sure to send them your YouTube video. Always ask for recommendations, and post these on your sites.

Audio samples are also great previews of what you offer as a speaker. When you do a teleclass or a radio interview, include a link to the audio on your Website. Choose a snappy segment of a teleseminar to keep it short, but be sure to showcase both your knowledge and your delivery style.

Promote Your Upcoming Events

Event planners also love speakers who help them put the word out about their events. When you contact groups to speak, be sure to mention if you've accumulated a large number of Facebook fans or Twitter followers. And if your opt-in newsletter list is in the thousands, it's also a terrific plus. Talk up the event and encourage your followers to attend for the chance to meet you in real life.

If you will be traveling, contact Meetup groups in the area and invite them to join you at your next event if the program is open to the public. If you can't invite them to the main event, see if they would like to do a coffee get-together with you during time in your travel schedule that would otherwise be wasted. You can also connect with the local chapters of national organizations of which you are a member or which pertain to your topic (groups such as eWomenNetwork, National Speakers Association, National Association of Women Business Owners, etc.) and issue the same invitations.

Don't forget to connect via the online groups on Facebook, LinkedIn, and Twitter for all of the same groups to invite them to attend and share tips related to your speech content. Talk about your upcoming programs on your own Facebook, Twitter, and LinkedIn pages, not from a hard sell, but in terms of the valuable content you're looking forward to sharing. You may find that some of your existing contacts will be in the area to attend, or have friends they can send your way.

Promote by Tweeting live from the event. Don't just Tweet about your part—let everyone know how much fun you're having, how valuable the speakers are, and what a great event it is. Tweet about the people you meet and the workshops you're attending. Take photos from your cell phone and upload them right away.

Promote after the event (great for being asked back again) by blogging, Tweeting, and uploading after you get home. (Make sure you've copied the organizer who invited you so he/she can see how much free publicity you've provided.) Write an article for your newsletter and then share it on your blog and in sound bites on your Twitter feed. Carry your digital video camera to the event and create a videoblog scrapbook, and then post it on YouTube. Tweet the link, add it to your other social media sites, and be sure to use social bookmarking to share it. When you send follow-up e-mails to the other attendees and speakers you met at the conference, include the links to your video and other promotions so they can also bask in the afterglow. Link to the organizers, speakers, and attendees you've met on Facebook, Twitter, and other sites, and choose the very best connections to add on LinkedIn.

Send a note to the speakers you met at the event extending that contact and offer to have them as a guest on your blog or podcast. Now you have another reason to talk. This can be a great way to share referrals to other possible speaking engagements or opportunities for collaboration for both of you. Of course, if you're hosting a guest on your site, that's yet another reason for social media promotion!

If you've got names for key contacts in the city to which you're traveling, whether they are reporters, radio hosts, or business contacts, look for them on Facebook, Twitter, blogs, and LinkedIn, and make a connection. Let them know you'll be in the area and would like to talk or meet for coffee. You can also marshal your LinkedIn contacts near your event city and ask them for referrals to local media or connections to the kinds of people you'd like to meet. Make your travel dollars stretch further by piggybacking extra mini-events or meetings onto your events.

Don't Overlook Online PR

Don't leave it up to the event organizers to publicize your upcoming appearances. When you book an engagement, write a press release and upload it to the many free online press-release distribution sites. Every release increases the number of places your name shows up in search engine results, and those links can help drive traffic to your site. Then Tweet the links to your releases, post them to the social bookmarking sites, and add them to your other Websites and social media pages.

You may also want to create a blog just for your news releases, and a separate blog for your upcoming appearances and have both feed into your Website and other social media pages. Doing so makes it easy and inexpensive for you to add to your releases and events without requiring a designer's help, keeps your schedule and news prominent and fresh on your sites, and makes your effort and links do triple duty.

When you're working the local media in the city where you'll be speaking, don't overlook locally based Internet radio shows, event-posting sites tied to the newspaper or zip code that allow you to upload the event announcement, and the load-your-own-news option now available on online newspaper, TV, and radio sites. You could cut your own inexpensive video news release (VNR) with a digital video recorder and a friend playing the anchor, make it look like a TV interview, and then upload it. (Note: The intent is to create an informative item in a news-like format, not to mislead the viewer to believe that they are watching a clip from an actual news show. Always attribute your company as the producer in the clip credits.)

Use your social media to find new ideas for events and bookings. Set Google Alerts not only for your own name, book titles, and company name, but use it to see what your competitors are doing. Add the names of the top five speakers in your topic or industry and see where they're speaking. That may give you new ideas for the local or regional chapters of the same organizations, or for a presentation that is similar but not repetitive to pitch to that group next year. If you subscribe to sites like eSpeaker.com or other online speakers bureaus, be sure to use the forums and member profiles to make your own connection to other speakers. Introduce yourself and forge alliances where you both share research, contacts, and tips about events. You can also use Facebook and LinkedIn to do the same with the speakers you meet at the conferences and events you attend.

Results Reminder

Social media offers a great chance to wow event planners before they ever pick up the phone.

The Rule of 30

What are 30 tips, video clips, audio sound bites, and free samples you can use on your social media sites to impress event planners and potential audiences?

30

Exercises

1. If you belong to online speakers' bureaus or professional speaking organizations, check out their sites' social media elements, such as online profiles, forums, and blogs. Make sure you take full advantage of these as part of your social media strategy.

2. View every social media opportunity as an audition for a new speaking engagement. Make the most of video and audio clips to let potential audiences see you at your best.

3. Make a list or create a calendar showing all your upcoming speaking engagements. Now use those events as the topic for blog posts and Tweets, incorporating them into your social media content strategy.

Social Media and Your Sales Funnel

29

Your sales funnel is the ever-narrowing path down which you lead people from being a prospect to becoming a customer, and from buying a low-priced item to purchasing your most expensive offerings.

A sales funnel is important because most people are not prepared to buy your most expensive product before they get to know you. The process of getting to know you involves those 30 touches that must connect with them when their need becomes urgent. Along the way, those 30 touches help a potential buyer learn to trust you and reassure themselves that you can help them solve their problem.

Social media provides cost effective ways to provide multiple connection points between prospects and your sales funnel. When a prospect encounters you in multiple places, you begin to work your way through the 30 touches and trust begins to build. Those touches turn into a relationship, and people buy from those with whom they have a relationship.

Down the Yellow Brick Road

Think about all of the products and services you offer. Grab a sheet of paper, and arrange those items from least to most expensive. Prospects are likely to try you out with the least commitment and expense before moving into a deeper relationship. If they like the first product, the most committed prospects will move further down your sales funnel to purchase a larger or more involved item, and the most motivated prospects who see a good fit reinforced through their previous purchases will become your big-ticket customers.

How many of your products or services (entry points to your sales funnel) do prospects encounter through your current social media sites? Here are some soft-sell ways to create visibility for your sales funnel while keeping the tone of your social media conversational:

~ Make sure that your online profile names you as the author/creator/provider of the products in your sales funnel. These could be books, home-study kits, CDs or DVDs, teleseminars, live events, or consulting services. Don't leave it up to readers to dig this information out of your Website.

~ Feature weekly tips from your books, classes, or information products, and credit the source.

~ Reference your books, classes, and events in a conversational manner as you blog and answer forum questions. Make it natural and avoid seeming contrived. Phrase the reference the way you would if you were having a face-to-face conversation.

~ Have your best introductory product listed in your e-mail signature and use that signature block when you answer forum questions.

~ Rotate free sample offerings. Those could include a single chapter from a book, a 15-minute snippet from a teleseminar, or part of a video from a live event.

~ Have at least a dozen bonus items that cost you nothing to provide via download (a great way to reuse articles, handouts, slide shows, or audio recordings) and offer these to social media friends and followers to increase their engagement in the funnel. Even better, build your opt-in mailing list by requiring an e-mail in order to provide fulfillment.

The Power of Mini-Events

Use the multimedia power of social networking sites to stage your own mini events to showcase your funnel. This is a great way to repurpose content you've already presented and created.

For example, invite your Facebook friends or Twitter followers to a one-day, online mini-event. You can have several short audio clips (no more than 10–15 minutes each), a downloadable handout, perhaps a short video (less than 10 minutes), and an online quiz or worksheet. Offer a free bonus item as a "thank-you" for attending. Promote the mini-event in advance and plan to be available live that day to answer questions on Twitter and/or Facebook.

You can also create a micro-event on Twitter by announcing that on a certain date and time, you'll be Tweeting content on a topic and taking live questions. Let everyone know in advance. Spice it up by doing a drawing (perhaps an e-book or a small downloadable product for which you normally charge a fee) from the names of the people who show up and interact during the event period.

You can also stage an online book launch and launch party via social media. Books are a great funnel-feeder, because they expose prospects to your knowledge, personality, and perspective at low cost and low risk to the buyer. If the reader likes the book, it's more tempting for them to delve deeper and get more products from you, moving down your sales funnel.

Talk up your new book and your publication date. Promote your online book launch party, and invite your e-mail list as well as your fans, friends, and followers to attend. Write a press release inviting the general public. Hold the launch party the day before the book becomes available in stores. You might even get your graphic designer to create digital party decorations, such as a banner, downloadable icons, or "signed" bookplates that attendees can download to put in their copy of the book.

Plan to offer a sneak peek of the first chapter, and make sure you have your cover art prominently displayed well in advance. Have your own photo visible as well, perhaps holding a copy of the book and cutting a cake in celebration. You could also showcase photos of yourself with your agent, publisher, or notable authors if you've done pre-launch live publicity events.

Create a video launch party greeting and post it for the party. You could even create party "favors" that are small graphic banners your guests can put on their own sites publicizing that they got the icon at your party. (What a great way to encourage viral marketing— by asking your guests to add a mini-banner/icon that clicks through to your sales page or Amazon link!) Plan to be live on your main social media sites during the party to greet guests, answer questions, and chat.

If you don't have a book, revise the book launch event to celebrate whatever new milestone you've recently attained. The point is to have fun and create a newsworthy and interactive reason for people to visit or revisit your sites.

Take Your Friends Behind the Scenes

Build interest in the products in your sales funnel by talking about how you create the books, teleseminars, live events, and other items you sell. People love to learn "how it's made," as TV shows on everything from cooking to construction attest. Blog or Tweet about the steps along the way and the process of writing, recording, or event planning. Talk about triumphs, setbacks, and frustrations.

Posts like these are still talking about your products, but in a non-sales way. Readers who follow you will begin to have an emotional investment in seeing the final product. They'll also be more likely to feel that a relationship has been created over the months where they've been a party to the inside scoop.

As you talk about the process of creating your products, you're also demonstrating credibility, responsibility, and expertise. You've also created a great opportunity to ask readers for what they'd like to see in the product and foster a two-way dialogue.

Another way to involve your readers with your sales funnel is to create an affiliate marketing structure to encourage and reward them for promoting your products to their own friends and opt-in list. Sites like Commission Junction (www.cj.com) make it easy to set up and manage your own affiliate program. Affiliates earn a percentage (usually 10–20 percent) of the price of the products they resell. Big-name experts who have large opt-in lists and thousands of readers require a larger percentage to promote affiliate products, but also offer more exposure. You'll need to provide marketing information for your affiliates so that they understand how to promote your products properly, but many experts who sell merchandise online have found affiliates to be a good way to expand their visibility. Commission Junction and other affiliate management sites also offer their own internal online communities where you can meet and network with other affiliates and entrepreneurs.

Results Reminder

Prospects prefer small steps on the way to larger purchases. Make it easy for them with a graduated progression of products and services visible through your social media.

The Rule of 30

Using the ideas in this chapter, what are 30 touches you could create to promote your sales-funnel products while maintaining a conversational, relationship-building style?

30

Exercises

1. Look at the list you made of your products or services in order from least to most expensive. Now make a second list matching each product to ideas for how to raise its visibility using social media.

2. Add your product launch dates to your master calendar of events and tie them into your online PR and social media content.

Beyond One Month: Where Do I Go From Here?

30

If you've applied the tactics in this book over the course of 30 days, congratulations! You've made a significant leap forward in promoting yourself, your business, and your products.

Take a moment to go back before you go further forward. Remember those prioritized business goals from the beginning of the book? Now is a good time to review your top one to three goals. Have your priorities changed? If so, reprioritize. Now rethink the target audiences linked to your top-priority business goal. Have you learned anything new about that audience as you've worked through the action items in this book? Make a note of it.

Short-Term and Long-Term Results

Thirty days of action will build you a strong new social media platform. To keep that momentum going and move further ahead requires a commitment to maintaining and extending what you've built for as long as it provides results.

You can't build it and walk away. The good news is that it's easier to maintain something that is up and functioning than to build it from scratch. You've also created a new habit of investing 30 minutes a day into creating and running your social media promotion. That habit will come in handy as you move forward from this point.

As with PR, advertising, and other promotion, social media takes time to deliver its full potential payback. Social media rewards people who are sincere in their interest to become a part of an ongoing community, and turns away from transients. As with a physical community, you have to invest time and effort to really become part of the neighborhood. People who get the best results from social media are sincerely interested in the online communities they've joined, and seek to make those groups a win-win for everyone involved.

If your initial 30-day goal was to create a powerful social media platform that has rich interconnections and an outreach to communities where your target audience is already well represented, then applying the action items in this book should help you create that result.

Now that you have your social media strategy in place, you have some choices to make on how you spend the next 30 days to move short-term results into long-term outcomes.

You may want to start by looking at the second- and third-priority business goals and folding them into your social media strategy. Or, you may want to tackle another type of marketing to get that element up and running while you maintain what you've built in social media. The 30-day approach can easily be applied to PR, personal networking, paid advertising, and other types of promotion. The key is to make sure your new steps leverage the visibility you've built with your existing social media platform to get the most effectiveness from your investment of time and money.

Find a New Jump-Off Point

By implementing what you've learned in this book, you can get your social media sites up and filled with valuable content. You've also learned how to reach out to qualified new friends, fans, and followers while also strengthening your connection to colleagues and business associates in the real world. You've built the building. The next step is to move in and get down to business.

As you remain engaged in social media, new sites with potential will catch your attention. New applications and widgets will create new opportunities to improve the way your pages communicate with readers. You'll see others doing innovative things with their social media and want to adapt those techniques to your own site. And, of course, month by month, you'll be adding new friends, fans, and followers through strategic friending and by connecting with the new people you meet in real life.

Maybe you didn't have the time during the first 30 days to do all of the things you wanted to do on social media. If that's the case, make a list of your next social media goals and use the 30 Day Results method to achieve your next set of goals.

This is also a good time to look for ways to better integrate your social media strategy with the rest of your promotional activities. If you haven't started a master calendar, now is a good time to begin. Get a large, blank calendar from an office supply store. Make sure it has plenty of room to write on each day, and choose a format that allows you to see at least three months at a time. Fill out your calendar by adding these items:

- Upcoming events you are hosting, both live and virtual.
- Speaking engagements.
- PR-worthy opportunities, such as product launches, book publications, or new locations.
- The days each week you regularly blog and Tweet.
- Any promotional specials you are planning to run.
- Holidays with tie-ins to your products or services.
- Paid advertisements already scheduled to run.
- Upcoming media interviews, guest blogging dates, or articles scheduled for submission.
- Upcoming awards, anniversaries, or other dates of significance.

Now think about how all these promotional opportunities can be leveraged through social media. Plan to use part of your ongoing

30 minutes a day to integrate these opportunities for visibility into your social media sites for maximum visibility. Keep your eyes open for new ways to add to your 30 Magic Touches as you develop additions to your products and services. And as you add new elements to your marketing mix, such as speaking or events, look for ways to integrate those efforts into your social media platform.

If you've decided to add another element of marketing to the mix in the next 30 days by using the 30 Day Results method, make sure you continue to keep at least two 30-minute periods per week for upkeep for your social media sites. Social media can't run on autopilot, and build-it-and-forget-it sites rapidly lose their fans and friends because of a lack of new content.

Lighten the Time Commitment With a Little Help From Some Friends

There's no magic bullet for promotion. It requires time and commitment, and provides best results when it has the opportunity to make an impact over the long run. That kind of ongoing obligation can seem scary, especially for small business owners and solo professionals. You can maximize your results and lighten the load by teaming up with colleagues and using a virtual assistant.

Blogs are a logical place to partner with other professionals who reach the same audience but with non-competing products or services. See if you can find several other people whom you respect professionally to become co-bloggers on a site you all share. Assign everyone their blogging day and spread the work around. The site remains fresh, readers get a variety of perspectives, and you only have to blog once a week instead of multiple times.

Virtual assistants (VAs) provide administrative help without being physically located at your office. You can find VAs on sites like Elance.com, Guru.com, and other online employment sites. Though you'll still need to write your blog posts and Tweets, and create your online content, a skilled VA can take the hassle of uploading the material off your hands, and help you clean off your Facebook wall, invite people who meet your strategic criteria to become your friend, fan, or follower, accept friend invitations, and respond to routine inquiries while keeping your pages free of spam and unwanted comments. Social media is a great task for a VA, because it can be accessed from anywhere. If you focus on creating quality content and overseeing the overall strategy, your VA can save you hours of uploading and free you to do the personal interaction side of your social media outreach.

Social media is a powerful, cost-effective addition to your marketing strategy. In today's world, business owners and solo professionals are notable by their absence if they're not utilizing social media. As you grow your business beyond your local area, social media can open doors to a global audience. By creating a way for professionals around the world to connect, share, sell goods and services, and develop relationships, it's clear that social media means business.

Want to Know More About Social Media?

The promotional possibilities of social media are changing daily. Gail Z. Martin speaks to live and virtual audiences with keynote presentations, seminars, and workshops to keep business owners and solo professional up-to-date on all the newest tools and techniques. Invite her to your next event. For those who want to go deeper, Gail offers online intensive group coaching programs and mastermind groups. Find out more at *www.GailMartinMarketing.com*.

Page 200 provides a calendar to help you during your 30 days to social media success. Use it to plan and track your progress.

1	2	3	4	5	6	7
8	9	10	11	12	13	14
15	16	17	18	19	20	21
22	23	24	25	26	27	28
29	30					

Index

A

B

About the Author

Gail Z. Martin is an author, entrepreneur, and international speaker on marketing for small business and solo professionals. She owns DreamSpinner Communications, the "Get Results" resource for affordable and effective small-business marketing, and works with companies, coaches, consultants, authors, speakers, and nonprofits throughout North America. Martin holds an MBA in marketing from the Pennsylvania State University, and has more than 25 years of marketing experience, including in corporate and nonprofit senior executive roles. She founded DreamSpinner Communications in 2003.

Martin speaks to international audiences on social media, small-business marketing, book promotion, and defining success. Whether it's a keynote presentation, workshop, seminar, or breakout session, Martin's high-energy, down-to-earth style energizes and provides a clear road to action.

Martin extends the strategies from her books through group-coaching programs, teleseminars, custom consulting, e-books, and home study programs. Learn more at *www.GailMartinMarketing.com*.

In addition to *30 Days to Social Media Success: The 30 Day Results Guide to Making the Most of Twitter, Blogging, LinkedIn, and Facebook*, Martin is also the author of *The Thrifty Author's Guide* series, which providers her unique approach to book marketing. Learn more at *www.ThriftyAuthor.com*.

Martin is the host of the Shared Dreams Marketing Podcast (*www.SharedDreamsPodcast.com*) where she interviews thought leaders, trendsetters, and notable entrepreneurs and authors. She's on Facebook as Gail Martin, and on Twitter as GailMartinPR. You'll also find her on Squidoo, MarketingProfs.com, 911MarketingHelp.com, SmartWomensCoaching.com, eWomenNetwork.com, and other sites specializing in small business and book marketing.

Martin is also the author of the best-selling fantasy adventure series *The Chronicles of the Necromancer* (*The Summoner, The Blood King, Dark Haven, Dark Lady's Chosen*) from Solaris Books and *The Fallen Kings* cycle from Orbit Books. Find her fiction online at *www.ChroniclesOfTheNecromancer.com*.

Martin lives in Charlotte, North Carolina, with her family.

Contact Gail Z. Martin at Gail@DreamSpinnerCommunications.com.